the Inner Chapel

Other Books by Becky Eldredge

Busy Lives & Restless Souls

*the*Inner Chapel

EMBRACING THE PROMISES OF GOD

BECKY ELDREDGE

LOYOLA PRESS.
A JESUIT MINISTRY
Chicago

LOYOLA PRESS.
A JESUIT MINISTRY

3441 N. Ashland Avenue
Chicago, Illinois 60657
(800) 621-1008
www.loyolapress.com

Scripture quotations contained herein are from the *New Revised Standard Version Bible: Catholic Edition*, copyright © 1993 and 1989 by the Division of Christian Education of the National Council of the Churches of Christ in the U.S.A. Used by permission. All rights reserved.

Cover art credit: Maria_Galybina/iStock/Getty Images, Artemisia1508/iStock/Getty Images.

ISBN: 978-0-8294-4933-4
Library of Congress Control Number: 2019957362

Printed in the United States of America.
20 21 22 23 24 25 26 27 28 29 Versa 10 9 8 7 6 5 4 3 2 1

To Boppy

I kept my promise. Thank you for loving me deeply and teaching me to love deeply. It opened me up to receive God's love and give it to others.

Contents

Find additional resources from Becky Eldredge
on prayer and other spiritual practices at

www.loyolapress.com/eldredge

beckyeldredge.com

PART 1

THE INNER CHAPEL

1

"Promise Me You'll Tell People That They Are Not Alone"

I knew something had changed when I realized I was the one holding the spoon. My grandmother lay flat on her back in the hospital bed, with only her head tilted. She was approaching the end of hour two of six following strict instructions to lie on her back as still as she could because of the excessive bleeding in the recovery room after her aortic-aneurysm surgery. I paused midscoop with the spoon that held her favorite treat, Blue Bell light vanilla ice cream, to peer into my grandmother's crystal-blue eyes. She and I held each other's gazes without speaking a word. During this long pause, we exchanged our love in silence. Love welled within me to the point of bursting as my blue eyes held the loving gaze of her blue eyes. How many times—from the days of my early childhood when she had spoon-fed me treats—had my eyes stared into hers and a deep understanding come over me that I was loved, deeply loved. Today, the same exchange was made, except I was the one holding the spoon. As I finished scooping the bite of ice cream, I glanced at her hands that told a thousand stories of gentle acts of kindness and love. Those hands had scooped bites of baby food into my mouth, stirred the large spoon in the cast-iron pot as she stood at her stove making a roux or crawfish étouffée, and joyfully fed her great-grandchildren the very treat I was feeding her today. She sheepishly accepted my offer of the bite of ice cream, the role reversal apparent to her as much as to me. She smiled and joked about this being her job when I was little.

I had no idea that holding the spoon in my hand that day marked the beginning of a life-changing journey. Three weeks later, my grandfather learned that he had a brain tumor. Two days before his surgery to remove this tumor, I submitted the manuscript for my first book. A week after his surgery, my hometown, Baton Rouge, experienced a flood that local news reporters called the thousand-year flood. The waters rose so quickly and suddenly that no one was prepared for the impact. My husband, brother, and uncle rescued my parents out of their home by boat. It was only a day later that we maneuvered our way through the wet, devastated streets of Baton Rouge to meet with my grandfather's neurosurgeon in New Orleans, to receive the news that the tumor they removed was indeed cancer: glioblastoma. After I'd spent hours on the Internet prior to this appointment, researching the possibilities, that word—*glioblastoma*—hit me in the stomach and literally took my breath away. Aggressive, terminal brain cancer.

We drove back through the water-soaked streets of Baton Rouge to my home. I could not process all that we were holding in this moment. The uncertainty of whether my parents' home was destroyed. The devastation of thousands of homes flooded around us, including those of neighbors, family, and friends. The people immediately in front of me needing help. The continued recovery of my grandmother from a life-threatening aortic aneurysm. The news of my grandfather's terminal cancer. I tried to wrap my head around the enormity of all that had happened in just a month's time while my mind raced through the various roles and responsibilities related to the calls of my life. Marriage. Motherhood. Ministry.

If I'm honest, I don't even know if I prayed that day in the car. I was overwhelmed to the point of feeling numb. The prayers came, though, in the days, weeks, and months after that car journey through my town. I cried out to God like never before as Baton Rouge fought its way through recovery again, as my grandmother healed, and as I accompanied my grandfather to his final breath.

So, here I am a few years later, writing this book. You might ask why. Why did I open with this story? It's simple, really. I believed in what this book was about long before the moment I realized I was the one holding the spoon. God began to awaken my understanding about it through life experience and witnessing the magnificent work of God in others through my ministry work.

Today, though, my belief in what you are about to read is not superficial or shallow. It is a bone-deep knowing, hard earned. It is a felt, whole-body belief in the gift of the inner chapel and in the promises of God.

The promises of God discussed in this book were included in one of the last conversations my grandfather and I had. He had the same blue eyes that my grandmother has. He stared up at me from his hospice bed on his sun porch, both of us knowing how little time we had left together. We shared words of love and thanksgiving. Then our conversation turned to how God is with us and how much God was with him. He was deeply thankful for the gift of never being alone, for being loved deeply, and for God's companionship throughout his journey.

We locked our blue eyes and exchanged a loving gaze, just as I had with my grandmother eighteen months earlier. The depth of my love for him and the gift of being deeply loved by him welled up and released a sob. Tears streamed down my face and his as he asked me to make him a promise. I nodded and called him by my special name for him: "Boppy, what is it?" Then, calling me by his special name for me, he said, "Becksa, promise me you'll tell people what we understand about God's love. Promise me you'll tell people that they are not alone. Promise me you will not stop what you are doing and will keep sharing the Good News with others."

This book is the fulfillment of the promise I made to Boppy. In so many ways, what lies in this book has been in me for years. It wasn't until I faced a stripping away of all certainty and walked closely with someone facing his death that I developed some clarity about what it all meant.

My prayer and hope for each of you as you read this is that you understand in a bone-deep, knowing way what my grandfather understood on his deathbed and what I came to understand in a deeper way as the spoon holder: There is an exquisite gift given to each of us—the inner chapel. And visiting it often allows us to discover the promises of God.

Spiritual Growth Is Like
Stepping into the Ocean

Every summer our family takes a trip to the beach, a tradition that began long before the kids were born but that is now a cherished family ritual. One of my favorite things to do as a mom is to watch our three children at the beach. Through the years I've watched the kids go from being barely able to sit up in the sand to crawling around eating sand, to the glorious year they can stand on their feet and put their toes in the water. With each passing year, their physical development and their courage allow them to enter deeper and deeper into the ocean. Where once they stayed close to shore with only inches of water covering their legs, my son, Brady, and my daughter Abby now head to waters deeper than their bodies can stand in. Our younger daughter, Mary, still likes to stay close to the shore where her feet solidly touch the ground.

As a mom, I sometimes stand on the sandy shore fiercely watching my older two as they make stroke after stroke in the waters where their feet do not touch the bottom. At times I want to call them back because of how deep they are willing to go. Sometimes, to be honest, I do just that because the fear of how deep the water is overwhelms me.

Other times I take a deep breath and try to remember that they both know the water's movements, and they have the skills to not only survive but also to thrive and enjoy the swim. The hours they've spent in the water along with their confidence in their own swimming abilities help them have a healthy respect for and joy from what these bodies of water provide. No matter their age or physical development, it's as if they are drawn in an unspoken way into the waters. It is almost as if something beckons them to enter the ocean.

Our relationship with God in prayer reminds me of watching my children on the beach. Our prayer lives begin with us on the sandy shore with Jesus at our side, just thrilled to be with us. He is there whether or not we are aware that he longs to be in relationship with us. At some point, we perceive his presence. I can imagine him standing with us on the beach, pointing into the ocean of endless possibilities of our relationship with God and asking us, *Are you ready to go into the waters? Do you want to go deeper?* Even though Jesus is right there with us, pointing the way, it is also as if the ocean of spiritual possibility beckons us to enter, awakening in us that same desire to put out into the deep as the ocean does my kids when they swim. It reminds me of the line in the Psalms, "Deep calls to deep" (Psalm 42:7). This beckoning and searching we feel is the Holy Spirit inviting us and drawing us ever deeper into our relationship with God. This deep-down desire is just one of many indications that God longs for us.

When we first enter the waters of relationship with God, we are similar to my kids when they could barely sit up on the beach without help. The waters of faith may feel both exciting and scary. We need extra support in our beginning moments of faith, no different from my hands firmly and lovingly holding my babies by their armpits so they could sit up on the beach. I would guess that most of us have had teachers and those who modeled for us how to pray.

Perhaps we have been immersed in a faith community that held us up in our relationship with God through the liturgical and communal life, wrapping around and supporting us through the spoken, memorized and communal prayers. As time progresses, we have become more familiar with living a life of faith. While Jesus never leaves our side, we might not need the extra support we did initially, just as when my kids' legs strengthened and I could hold their hands as they became more sure-footed but were not yet ready to stand on their own two feet by themselves. The journey of faith is a steady invitation to deeper water. While we are always accompanied by Jesus, we become surer of our footing as we progress along the way.

At some point, though, we feel surer of what it means to live a life of faith, and as Jesus invites us to go deeper, we are more comfortable saying yes as we lean more and more on the practices—skills, tools—of our faith. My kids developed to the point of being sure enough to stand on their own feet. When they were at this point, my husband or I would point to the water with excitement and ask them, "Do you want to go into the water?" Our oldest child, our son, answered this question with the physical response of letting go of our hands and barreling full force into the water, his feet stumbling as the sandy slope and gravity pulled his top-heavy head in first. Even his fall did not keep him from wanting to stay in the water. Our middle daughter said yes but wanted to keep holding our hands as she put in first her toes and got used to how the ocean felt as it wrapped around her body. It took hours before she was willing to let go of our hands. Our younger daughter, despite the example of her two older siblings, who effortlessly played in the water before her, took some convincing to give the ocean a try. Within minutes of entering, though, she released our hands and splashed and ran happily in the shallow waters, still mindful that there was a place that was too deep for her comfort.

I watch people enter the waters of faith in similar ways: sometimes timidly entering their prayer lives, putting in only one toe at a time. Some yearn to cling to a hand of support for a long time until they feel comfortable. Other times, people are so ready to enter that they barrel in with such excitement they almost trip all over themselves as they enter the ocean of God's love and mercy, the way my son stumbled and fell into the ocean.

There are two important things for us to remember about this invitation from Jesus to enter the waters of faith. First, he never leaves our side. We are always accompanied by him. Second, he is always inviting us to go deeper, eventually drawing us into water where we can no longer touch the bottom, and we are invited to even go under and swim in the quiet waters below the surface. No matter where we are in our faith journey, there is more to learn and explore in our relationship with God.

LET'S GO TO THE INNER CHAPEL

The "inner chapel" is simply a place within each of us where God dwells and where we can meet God. As we move through this book, you will learn more details about what it means to go to the inner chapel. For now, let's begin with a short reflection.

Perhaps at this moment you are standing in ankle-deep or knee-deep water. Maybe you've taken steps further out, and you are up to your shoulders and head. Maybe you are even at the point that your feet do not touch the bottom anymore, and you are swimming in deeper water, trusting both God's movement in your life and learning new practices of our faith that support your ever-growing relationship with God.

One thing is for certain. It's amazing to know that no matter where we are on this "ocean adventure," we are not alone. We are supported. We are accompanied. Jesus is with us. We are even being prayed for by the Holy Spirit to help us enter the water or swim deeper.

Ocean Reflection

I invite you right now to pause and bring to mind the image of an ocean. Where are you in your relationship with God? Are you standing on the sandy shore with Jesus beside you, inviting you in? Are you in inch-deep water? Up to your ankles? Knees? Shoulders? In water so deep that you are not able to touch the ocean floor?

Notice where you are. At the same time, where do you feel the magnetic pull of the Holy Spirit inviting you to go? Where do you feel God inviting you to go? Where do you notice Jesus pointing you and showing you the way?

Notice, too, where you feel you *want* to go. Do you want to say yes to their invitation? Perhaps you want to turn and run back along the familiar path you've been on and return to the safety of shore, as both of our girls did at first when they entered the ocean. Wherever you are, it is okay. Wherever you are at this moment, there are also two things to remember. God is with you right where you are. And God is inviting you and wants you to go deeper.

I'm reminded of the Gospel story in which Jesus invites his disciples to toss nets by "putting out into the deep" (Luke 5:4). How are you experiencing God inviting you to "put out into the deep"? No matter where you are, know that there are prayer practices to support you—where you are and also where God is inviting you to go.

Embracing the Promises of God

These Scriptures can encourage you as you read them and pray with them.

- Psalm 42:1–7 // "As a deer longs for flowing streams, so my soul longs for you, O God. My soul thirsts for God, for the living God."
- Luke 5:1–11 // Jesus invites Simon to put his nets out into the deep.
- Jeremiah 29:11–14 // "For surely I know the plans I have for you, says the LORD, plans for your welfare and not for harm, to give you a future with hope. Then when you call upon me and come and pray to me, I will hear you. When you search for me, you will find me; if you seek me with all your heart, I will let you find me."

3

The Gift of the Inner Chapel

My desire for God awakened in the middle of my high school life that was full of family, friends, school, dating, socializing, and looking forward to the future. God initiated a relationship with me by grabbing my heart during junior year of high school and awakening a longing that sent me searching for something to satisfy that longing and make it stop. It took me a while to understand that what I was longing for was a relationship with God, and it was this growing desire to deepen my relationship with God that sent me tenaciously searching for more in college. During college, I attended several retreats and youth/young-adult conferences, participated in multiple Bible studies, and dabbled in an array of campus ministries on LSU's (Louisiana State University) campus. Each of these events or programs I attended left me on a "spiritual high," but shortly after I returned to normal life, the high would come crashing down, and I found myself aimless as to how to sustain what I had experienced during a retreat or conference or Bible study. What I felt reminded me of Peter at the Transfiguration, begging Jesus to stay on the mountaintop. I wanted to stay on the mountaintop and savor my experience of God. The cycle would repeat. I would attend a retreat or event that filled my tank and fueled my hunger for God even more. I would return home, and days later the crash would hit, and I found myself lost, aimless, and searching again. There was a hunger in me that felt as if it could never be satisfied, despite my efforts to grow my relationship with God through continued attendance at various programs.

Maybe you feel like this now or have felt it in the past.

When I Discovered the Inner Chapel

I sat in the church at Christ the King Parish on LSU's campus during the fall semester of my junior year at the 8:00 p.m. Sunday Mass and heard an announcement about a Busy Person's Retreat. I heard *daily prayer, retreat,* and *spiritual director.* I did not fully grasp what these terms meant, but I noticed my heart responding and the insatiable longing burning within me again. It felt as if there was a string on my heart and someone was gently pulling on it, trying to get me to pay attention and say yes.

Curious to learn more about a Busy Person's Retreat, and hoping to calm my restlessness, I signed up for yet another retreat. When the organizer of the Busy Person's Retreat began to talk at the opening meeting, I learned that this retreat was different from others I had attended. As I listened to how this whole thing worked, I became a little nervous. I hadn't done anything like this before. For starters, the retreat was not a large-group experience full of music, small-group discussions, presentations, and games. Instead, it consisted of meeting with a spiritual director one-on-one for thirty minutes a day for four days in a row. In addition, each day I would commit to daily prayer on my own. I was a tad anxious because I had no idea how to really implement daily prayer into my life. Minutes before that opening meeting ended, I almost changed my mind when I thought, *What in the world did I get myself into?*

After the opening meeting, I met my spiritual director for the retreat, Sr. Ily Fernandez, CSJ. Instantly, her smile and warmth put my worries at ease. We briefly shared a bit about ourselves and set a time for our first meeting the next day. She assigned me a Scripture passage to pray with before we met again. She also shared some guidance on how to set up a daily prayer time and how to pray with Scripture. Over the next four days, we met one-on-one. During our time together she asked me about my relationship with God and what touched me about the Scripture I prayed with. She continued to encourage me to have a daily prayer time. She helped me discern how to make prayer time fit around my college schedule and within the reality of living in a very small room with a roommate ten feet away from me. At the end of our daily time together, she assigned me a new Scripture to pray with during my next prayer time.

As the retreat progressed, I noticed something changing. The intense longing for more that never quite went away seemed to dissipate when I went to that place of quiet—inside and outside—to pray this way. The fifteen to twenty minutes of silence I took in the middle of college life to pray with Scripture not only stilled my mind but also stilled and expanded my heart. During the last meeting of my retreat, Sr. Ily encouraged me to continue on this path of prayer by taking time every day for prayer. She suggested that I continue using Scripture during my prayer time. I now understand that she invited me to go daily to my inner chapel.

We continued to meet monthly for spiritual direction for a few years after we first met on the Busy Person's Retreat. Writing this, it overwhelms me to think about how she guided me. Sr. Ily, who is still a very dear friend of mine, not only opened me to spiritual direction but also taught me how to pray in daily life. While we never used the words when we met, she is the one who first showed me to the inner chapel and taught me how to access this beautiful gift from God in the middle of my life.

My first Busy Person's Retreat changed the trajectory of my life. I can follow the thread from that experience to this current moment, in which I am now a spiritual director and colleague of Sr. Ily's, often working side by side with her as we accompany others on their faith journeys the way she did me all those years ago. What she first taught me when I was twenty continues to impact my relationship with God, my marriage, my motherhood, my ministry—my entire life, really.

The greatest comfort and hope of my life is this gift of the inner chapel. Without it, I would be lost and still searching like crazy for the next thing to bring me a spiritual high or the next thing to satisfy my longing. My strength is *within*. It's not my willpower or my personal drive or gumption, but some*one*: God within me, who is readily available at any given moment. Here, in my inner chapel, I meet God and experience the promises that come with this ever deepening relationship.

This is what I want you to know: The gift of the inner chapel that Sr. Ily taught me is within each one of us. It is a place where we can come to understand not only our longing for God but also God's longing to be in relationship with us.

We each have an inner chapel, a space within us where God resides. This means that at any point in our day we have a sacred space where we can pause for prayer. It is a space to which only you and God have access. This means we can call on God at any moment, no matter what we are doing. It is where we meet God, get to know Jesus, and learn the ways the Holy Spirit works in our lives.

My inner chapel is the safest place I know. It is shelter within, a true sanctuary in my heart. It is a place I can say anything, share with and show God anything. I can share with God more than any other person in my life, even Chris, my husband. It is a place that feels comfortable and familiar. In this sacred space, God has detailed knowledge of me—just as God has detailed knowledge of you in your inner chapel.

This sacred space within us is not a new thing. For centuries, characters of our salvation history have leaned on the strength of the inner chapel. In the Old Testament, we find examples such as Abraham, who sits at the entrance of his tent to meet God (Genesis 18:1). God invites him to come look at the stars and promises him that his descendants will be as numerous as the stars (Genesis 15:4–6). Moses spends forty days and forty nights on top of a mountain with God. It is in this space that God reveals the Ten Commandments and the details of the Ark of the Covenant. Time with God leaves Moses so radiant he has to cover his face with a veil when with other people (Exodus 34:27–35). Although Abraham and Moses both went to specific physical spaces to meet God, God opened their hearts to intimate conversation; you might say that Abraham's sky and Moses's mountain represented the interior space where God speaks with each of us.

Jesus gives us a multitude of examples of his going away to be with God in the quiet of his heart. His transfiguration was one of these times, and here are a few other examples.

- **Jesus withdrawing to pray for a night.** "Now during those days he went out to the mountain to pray; and he spent the night in prayer to God" (Luke 6:12).
- **Jesus finding a deserted place to pray in the morning.** "In the morning, while it was still very dark, he got up and went out to a deserted place, and there he prayed" (Mark 1:35).
- **Jesus withdrawing to pray in the evening.** "And after he had dismissed the crowds, he went up the mountain by himself to pray. When evening came, he was there alone" (Matthew 14:23).

The legacy of men and women leaning on the strength of their inner chapels to grow in relationship with God continues from Jesus to the apostles and the early church, to the long array of saints who went before us. They leave us glimpses of their wisdom about how to access and draw on the resources of the inner chapel. We learn from St. Catherine of Siena's image of the inner cell, St. Teresa of Ávila's wisdom in the interior castle, and St. Thérèse of Lisieux sharing how "Jesus teaches me in secret" and how "the Kingdom of God is within me at each moment."[1] St. Ignatius of Loyola spent his whole ministry life teaching others how to access what he learned about growing an intimate relationship with God through his personal experiences within the cave of Manresa. Perhaps one of my favorite quotes on the value of silence and prayer comes from St. Mother Teresa:

> "God is the friend of silence. His language is silence." Be still and know that I am God. He requires us to be silent to discover him. In the silence of the heart, he speaks to us. . . . We need silence to be alone with God, to speak to him, to listen to him, to ponder his words deep in our hearts. We need to be alone with God in silence to be renewed and to be transformed. Silence gives us a new outlook on life. In it we are filled with the grace of God himself, which makes us do all things with joy.[2]

These holy men and women who came before us offer us shoulders to stand on and provide a model of how to rely on our inner chapels in today's world and within today's realities. What God revealed to them is not static and stuck in time; rather, it is ever changing and unfolding as our world changes and cultures change. Even today, while our

---

1. John Clarke, O.C.D., *The Story of a Soul: The Autobiography of St. Thérèse of Lisieux* (Washington, D.C.: ICS Publications, 1996), 276, 294.
2. Mother Teresa, *Total Surrender*, rev. ed., ed. Brother Angelo Devananda (Kolkata, India: Missionaries of Charity, 1985), 101.

worlds are drastically different, we can incorporate the inner chapel into daily life as Abraham, Jesus, and so many saints did before us.

The Inner Chapel Today

There's no doubt that the pace of our culture continues to get busier and faster. Our days are cramped with appointments, commitments, and to-do lists. I watch as my own family and others around me seem to leave home earlier in the morning and return later in the evening as we attempt to make more time to accomplish all that we need to do. This rapid pace, along with all the turmoil, violence, and division happening in our world can leave us feeling awfully restless and even hopeless.

I believe there is a need more than ever to invite people to embrace the inner chapel and encourage people to grow an intimate relationship with God. Rather than forget the promises of God, our world needs to cling to them as never before. The good news is not only that the promises of God exist but also that we can go to our inner chapels every day, despite our own busyness and the world's chaos, and meet God within us.

LET'S GO TO THE INNER CHAPEL

Creating a Spiritual Autobiography

A guiding principle in Ignatian spirituality is looking backward over your spiritual journey in order to better shape and understand where you are going. I invite you to create your own spiritual autobiography using these questions as a guide.

- What was your first awareness of God? When and where was your first "inner chapel" experience? What was your experience of God then? What were your reactions?
- What were other ordinary or extraordinary experiences of God in your inner chapel? When and where did they take place; who or what was God like; what, if any, reactions did you have to those experiences?
- Where have you had a sense of God at work in your life? How did God work—through a big moment of revelation or gradually, in small, quiet moments?
- What has your search for God looked like? What desires do you feel stirring within you now?
- What has your journey of prayer looked like? When did your prayer life begin?
- How would you describe your inner chapel now?
- What retreats, events, and programs have fostered your own spiritual growth?

Embracing the Promises of God

These Scriptures can encourage you as you read them and pray with them.

- Matthew 17:1–8 // Jesus' transfiguration
- Matthew 7:7–8 // "Ask, and it will be given you; search, and you will find."
- Psalm 17:6–7 // "I call upon you; for you will answer me, O God."
- Psalm 46:10 // "Be still, and know that I am God."

Prayers and Recipes, Teachers and Cooks

Let's turn now to how we can learn the art of praying and going to our inner chapel every day. It reminds me of how I learned to make crawfish étouffée from my grandmother.

Learning the Art of Cajun Cooking

One of the best cooks in the world is my grandmother. She was raised in Louisiana. Some of my favorite childhood memories are of walking into my grandparents' home and being greeted by the sight of my grandmother cooking and the smell of one of her dishes simmering on the stove. Roast and homemade gravy. Spaghetti with ground beef. Meat loaf with tomato sauce. Red beans and rice. And the holy grail dish: my grandmother's crawfish étouffée.

When my grandmother cooked étouffée, I hovered around her at the stove, eagerly waiting for her to give me permission to grab a small spoon, lift the lid of her cast-iron Dutch oven, and sample a flavor of the hidden goodness inside. That little taste of it left me hungering for more. I would beg her for another taste, and she would often give in to my pleas for one more but then cut me off by closing the lid and saying, "You have to wait until dinner for the rest." It felt like an eternity waiting for dinnertime with the delicious smell hitting my nostrils and the lingering taste of heavenly goodness on my tongue.

During my first year of marriage, I wanted to learn how to make my grandmother's étouffée so Chris and I could not only enjoy the dish but also begin creating memories and traditions like those I'd experienced as a child. I asked my grandmother to write down her recipe for crawfish étouffée. This is what she wrote:

> Onion, bell pepper, and celery
> Butter
> Flour
> A few Mardi Gras size cups of water
> Make a roux.
> Add your crawfish tails.
> Cover top of pot with pepper and salt and Tony's (a Cajun seasoning).
> Season to taste.

I read the recipe and chuckled. "Grandmother, you don't have the amounts listed! How much do I do of each?"

Her reply: "A certain amount."

A certain amount? "How in the world am I going to figure it out?"

She told me, "Don't worry. You'll figure it out."

Confident that I had watched her make the dish enough times and I had tasted it during the cooking process, I went home determined to make this for our dinner.

I pulled out my heirloom cast-iron Dutch oven, given to us when we got married, and began to gather ingredients. I warmed up the pot on the stove just as I'd watched my grandmother do a million times. When it was good and hot, I put in the "Cajun trinity"—onion, celery, and bell pepper—at the bottom, along with a stick of butter. As I surveyed my sautéing vegetables, I felt pretty confident that I was going to do just fine. As the vegetables began to wilt, I looked at the recipe and saw that flour was next. Not having any idea what a "certain amount" of flour for a crawfish étouffée roux looked like, I scooped a cup of flour into the pot and began making the roux. Knowing that you don't want to add the water until the color is right, I continued to stir, hoping that it would get to peanut-butter color. I asked the question every Cajun cook asks when making a roux: is it time to add the water yet?

Looking at Grandmother's recipe again, I saw that it called for "a few Mardi Gras size cups of water." Only in Louisiana would a recipe read like this! I went to my kitchen cabinets that held the special "Louisiana china" of plastic Mardi Gras cups caught from the Mardi Gras parades I'd attended. Which size should I use? The large one from Endymion? The small lime-green one from Southdowns parade in Baton Rouge? The medium-size one that we got at a truck parade last year on Mardi Gras Day? Too embarrassed to call my grandmother, I grabbed the large one and filled it with water from the kitchen sink. Taking a deep breath, I poured the water into the roux and began to stir frantically, making sure it didn't stick to the pot. As the steam evaporated away, I was able to peek at my roux's color. It was anything but peanut-butter color. It resembled more what mashed-up mushrooms would look like—whitish gray.

I was crestfallen. Determined that it was still edible, I went ahead and added a bit more water to the pot and then threw in the crawfish tails. As the sauce and tails came to a boil, I read Grandmother's next step. Cover the pot with salt, pepper, and Tony's. Not wanting to deviate from the recipe too much, I heavy-handedly covered the pot's contents with salt, pepper, and Tony's. To be honest, there was a pretty thick layer of pepper. I brought it to a boil and let it simmer.

Finally, the time came to give it a taste. I grabbed a spoon, lifted the pot lid, and—feeling the same excitement I'd experienced before tasting Grandmother's dish when I was a child—dipped in the spoon and put it in my mouth. In about two seconds, I ran to the sink and spat it out. It was unbelievably disgusting. The consistency of the roux was awful. The taste was horrific. The heat of the spices continued to burn my throat.

Ashamed at my failure in Cajun cooking, I sheepishly dialed my grandmother. She answered the phone with hopeful anticipation. "Well, how does it taste? I've been waiting to hear!" I nearly burst into tears telling her how awful it was. In her kind, gentle way, she encouraged me and said, "You know what? Why don't you come over tomorrow? You bring your pot. I'll have mine. I'll cook a batch in my pot, and you can watch as I do. At the same time, you can cook in your pot. I'll be right there to help you." Feeling a bit deflated, I agreed to our next day's lesson of making étouffée.

I walked into my grandparents' house, carrying my cast-iron pot. My grandmother had all the ingredients ready for my second try and for her umpteenth try. Hers to the left of the stove. Mine to the right. After a few minutes of warm greeting, Grandmother invited us to get to work.

Before standing side by side at her stove, I grabbed a piece of paper and a pen to take notes. I placed my pot next to hers on the burners. We both turned on a burner and chatted a bit while the pots heated up. When the pots were ready, Grandmother grabbed her stick of butter and placed it in the bottom of the pot to begin melting. I did the same. Then she grabbed her bag of frozen Cajun trinity and poured a "certain amount" in her pot. She invited me to do the same and then told me when the "certain amount" was the right amount. We stood side by side sautéing the vegetables. When it was time to add the flour, she grabbed her canister of flour and scooped out a "certain amount." I mirrored what she did but *measured* my flour before it went into the pot.

We both began the rhythmic stirring of roux making. I watched her pot and my own, looking to see how her consistency was compared to mine. We stirred and talked as we watched the roux slowly turn the right color of peanut butter. Finally, she said, "We are ready for the water."

I watched as she grabbed her well-worn "measuring cup" for water: a small, white Mardi Gras cup so used that you could no longer make out the ink or writing on it. She filled it up, and before she poured it in, I grabbed a liquid measuring cup to note the amount before she poured it in her pot, and then I did the same.

When the steam cleared, I saw I had a beautifully colored and smooth sauce in my pot. Grandmother whooped with joy, and so did I. My grandfather, too, let out a holler of support. Knowing then that the hardest part of the dish was behind me, we continued. We added the crawfish tails and remaining seasonings in the pot and waited for the sauce to come to a boil. We continued to stand beside each other, tasting, stirring, and adjusting the seasoning until it was just right and ready to eat.

That night, my husband met me at my grandparents' house and the four of us sat down at their kitchen table that I love so much, and we ate from both of our batches of crawfish étouffée. I left Grandmother's house that night knowing I could make crawfish étouffée and try it again with confidence. I did it the next week on my own, and I have cooked dozens of batches of crawfish étouffée since. Now my own three children enjoy this delicious Cajun dish.

It wasn't too long ago that my son, who loves to cook, asked me if I could teach him how to make crawfish étouffée. I decided that instead of giving him a written recipe, I would teach him the art of Cajun cooking as my grandmother had taught me: side by side.

Recipe for Prayer

Learning how to pray can feel much like learning how to make crawfish étouffée. There is not one secret recipe. You learn a few foundational basics, and then you learn to taste, tweak, and season based on where God has you on your faith journey. Let's take a peek now at a few of the fundamental basics of prayer and how to visit your inner chapel every day.

In Louisiana cooking, many dishes, such as crawfish étouffée, begin with the "trinity." No, I am not referring to the Father, the Son, and the Holy Spirit. Instead, this trinity includes onion, celery, and bell pepper. From these three ingredients, a wide array of Cajun dishes is made: gumbo, jambalaya, crawfish étouffée, red beans and rice, and shrimp creole, among many others.

In our prayer lives, there is a "trinity" that is essential as well: our time of prayer, our place of prayer, and our space of prayer. If we want to access the resources of the inner chapel, we need to lean in to an intentional prayer time. I invite you to reflect on these three questions and how you can implement them in your life.

1. When can be your time of prayer?
2. Where can be your place of prayer?
3. How can you make it a sacred space?

The cooking trinity gives foundational flavor to Cajun dishes; without the base, Cajun dishes lose their robust flavors. The three elements of prayer give foundation to a long-term, sustainable prayer life.

The flavor of our prayer lives comes by the way God is inviting us to spend time together in our inner chapels. This reminds me of asking various South Louisiana cooks how to make a gumbo, another treasured Cajun dish. The base ingredients of the trinity will be listed no matter who is cooking the gumbo; however, from there, the list of ingredients will vary greatly. Some may cook a gumbo with sausage and chicken, while others make a seafood variation, and others do a duck and andouille sausage. Besides varying the protein in the gumbo, there will be a wide variety of seasonings unique to each cook, including additions such as okra, tomatoes, or filé (a spicy herb made from dried and powdered sassafras leaves).

There is an expansive list of prayer methods that we can bring into our foundational prayer time. Each is distinctive and offers a special way of relating to God. Part of our work of going to our inner chapel every day is discerning which prayer method God is inviting us to use. While the list is expansive, in this book we will look closely at how praying with Scripture can support us in going to our inner chapel on a daily basis and discovering the promises of God.

Let's turn now to other key ingredients for a long-term, sustainable prayer life. Once you have your foundational prayer time put in place, here are a few other helpful pointers to support your prayer life.

Begin your prayer. Once in your prayer place, intentionally place yourself in the presence of God. Take a few deep breaths. As you breathe in and out slowly, remind yourself that you are never alone and that God is with you right now.

Name the grace you seek. St. Ignatius invites us to name the grace we seek at the start of every prayer period. After placing yourself in the presence of God, simply go to God with the question, *What is the grace I seek?*

Notice what word arises in your mind and heart. Are you seeking rest? Peace? Clarity? Courage? Hope? Light? Love? Mercy? And on and on the list might go. When a word arises in your thoughts, turn this into a prayer:

"God, as I begin, I seek the grace of _____."

Then begin your prayer time using the prayer method God is inviting you to use at the moment.

Choose your prayer method. I will cover a few types of prayer methods later in the following chapters.

Review your daily prayer. At the end of your prayer time, St. Ignatius also invites us to do a review of prayer. This simply involves a look back over the minutes spent in prayer with the question *What happened here?*

It might be helpful to purchase a journal where you can jot down what you noticed in prayer. Perhaps you write the word or phrase from Scripture that caught your heart. Maybe you jot down a memory or image that God stirred in prayer. You might note the feelings that rose within you as you prayed. Did you feel hopeful? Sad? Frightened? Afraid?

Review your prayer weekly. As you continue to lean in to your intentional prayer time, you may also find it helpful to do a weekly review of prayer. This is similar to the daily review of prayer; to do a weekly review, you look back over your daily notes of prayer to jot down what has happened in this week's prayer time. The practice of reviewing prayer is a beautiful tool to help discern the movement of God within our hearts and also within our lives.

The art of looking backward and reviewing our prayer will help us continue our forward movement and growth in God.

Learning How to Pray

Our prayer lives often begin within a community or through some experience with others that awakens our desire for it and leaves us desiring more. It is not only about experiencing prayer but also about learning how to pray and, at some point, teaching others to pray.

My grandmother came alongside me to teach me how to cook. So many others came alongside me to teach me to pray. My parents modeled it in our home. My church community surrounded me with our common vocal prayer at Mass each Sunday. My Catholic school community in grade school and high school immersed me in prayer as we began class in prayer, as we opened the school in prayer, and as we prayed in the ritual of school Mass. In Catholic schools, I was encouraged, and—let's be honest—sometimes required, to memorize prayers. In high school, I was exposed to various prayer methods, including silence. In college, Sr. Ily taught me how to pray with Scripture. For the past two decades of my life, spiritual directors accompanied me in my journey of prayer, offering new prayer methods to try, teaching me not only how to pray but also how to discern. They helped me through dry seasons of prayer, seasons of consolation, and seasons of desolation. They helped me discern how to pray, even when I became a parent and the steady daily routine I once had needed to shift and shape around seasons of parenthood.

The bottom line is this. I have never been on my own in learning how to pray. I was supported not only by God in coming to my prayer time; I also had people along the way who came alongside me and still come alongside me to teach me how to pray. Many of these people were spiritual directors whose role in my life was to be holy listeners for an hour each month. They would help me listen to the movement of God in my inner chapel and in daily life. Even as I became more confident in prayer and did daily prayer on my own, I knew their accompaniment was available, and I leaned on it each month in spiritual direction. As God drew me deeper into relationship, these teachers offered me tools for prayer to continue to go to my inner chapel as the seasons of my prayer life changed. After twenty years of being accompanied by someone in spiritual direction, my toolbox for both prayer and discernment is packed with a variety of resources available to me at any moment in my inner chapel. Even today as I accompany others, I continue to choose to be accompanied by someone each month in spiritual direction.

So, while my own journey of prayer has led me to write about and teach others how to pray, I am still a student of prayer, living out my commitment to daily prayer, all the while teaching others how to pray.

We Are All Both Cooks and Teachers

In the school of prayer and developing our interior life, we are students and cooks and also teachers. We tend to believe that in some fields of expertise, you reach a certain level of skill or experience and then you stop doing the skill and move solely into teaching and sharing the wisdom of how to do the skill you've mastered. But masters in any field, whether playing an instrument or practicing medicine, will say that they never stop learning. In prayer, our schooling never stops. We have to be practitioners of the very thing we are also called to teach others. Being a person of prayer means that we are not only still cooking but also still learning. We, too, even at a later stage of our spiritual lives, still need someone to come alongside us and accompany us. At the same time that we are praying and being accompanied, we are called to accompany someone else and teach them.

So, I invite you first and foremost to embrace the gift of the inner chapel in your own life. From my experience, I believe you will discover it to be a steady respite in the busyness of life and also a constant source of hope, comfort, love, and mercy.

LET'S GO TO THE INNER CHAPEL

Learning How to Pray: Reflection

Think about your own life.

- Who taught you how to pray?
- Who modeled for you how to pray?
- Who is teaching you now?
- Who is modeling for you now?
- Who is accompanying you right now?
- Do you seek to have someone accompany you in your prayer life?
- Whom are you invited to teach how to pray?

Creating a Spiritual Plan

- When can be your time of prayer?
- Where will your place of prayer be?
- How can you make it a sacred space?
- Do you seek to have a spiritual director accompany you in your prayer life?

Embracing the Promises of God

These Scriptures can encourage you as you read them and pray with them.

- 1 Thessalonians 5:17–18 // "Pray without ceasing."
- Matthew 6:9–15 // "Pray then in this way."
- Romans 8:26–27 // "The Spirit helps us in our weakness."
- Hebrews 4:15–16 // "Approach the throne of grace."

5

Practical Prayer from St. Ignatius of Loyola

Our Christian faith holds the common invitation to be in relationship with God. Within the various spiritualities of Christianity, multiple expressions have emerged of what faith in God looks like. I want to share with you a way of being in the world and living your faith. This is a way I am grateful someone cared enough to teach me. More than just a someone—several people, actually. Embracing this way of being and living changed my life. It continues to do so. It offers me a way forward despite what's going on in the world. It is a way that keeps me on the path of hope, in relationship with God. I am talking about the Ignatian way.

Ignatian spirituality is one of many spiritualities that are part of the two-thousand-year-old path of Jesus. Throughout the centuries, God revealed to various women and men, most of whom are now saints, certain ways to be in relationship with God. These developed into spiritualities. Each spirituality has unique elements and practices for relating to God. St. Ignatius of Loyola and those who helped him form the Society of Jesus (the Jesuits) developed the Ignatian way.

Other major schools of spirituality are Franciscan, Benedictine, Vincentian, Dominican, and Carmelite.

The spirituality I find my home in is Ignatian. It is the expression of the Christian Catholic faith I have lived most of my life. I didn't know this path had a name until my early twenties. When I finally understood that the ways in which I was naturally drawn to be in relationship with God had a name, I realized I was immersed in Ignatian spirituality for most of the faith formation in my youth. This was due to the Sisters of St. Joseph of Medaille educating me in grades kindergarten through twelve, their charism (ministry) being rooted in Ignatian spirituality.

I believe that the Ignatian way is one that busy laypeople can find a home in today. The elements and guiding principles of Ignatian spirituality resonate and can be practiced easily within the realities of everyday life. The entire spirituality is based on learning to live as a "contemplative in action," which simply means being a person of prayer who lives out a unique call in the world. The Ignatian prayer practices give guidance on how to become a more contemplative, reflective person. Ignatian discernment wisdom offers tools to discern among the multitude of choices we face.

My hope is to offer you an invitation and concrete steps to help you deepen your relationship with God by living the Ignatian practices and using its tools. It is by living the Ignatian way of prayer, discernment, and action that I have come to discover the gift of the inner chapel and the promises of God and what they mean to my daily reality.

The Ignatian way is not just for priests, religious brothers, or religious sisters but is a path for laypeople, too. Nor is this spirituality available only when you reach a certain stage of life and "things slow down," as I have been told more times than I can count. The Ignatian way is available to us right now as we are, where we are, no matter what stage of life we are in. It does not matter whether

- you are young or old, single, married, or divorced;
- you have kids or do not have kids;
- you are in the throes of raising young children or accompanying your young tweens, teenagers, or young adults;
- your children are single adults, married adults, divorced adults, or parents themselves; or
- you are not working, starting to work, in the long years of the great big middle of work, or in retirement.

The path is prayer, and the time is now.

Ignatian Prayer Practices

Ignatian spirituality offers several prayer practices that can be incorporated easily into daily life. We will look at some of these in depth throughout the book. For now, here is a brief overview of some Ignatian prayer practices.

- **Reviewing our prayer and experience.** We will learn prayer practices that help us look backward over our day, our week, and our experiences to better understand God's work in our lives and where we are heading now.
- **The *Examen*.** This tool helps us pray our life and grow our awareness that we are not alone.
- **Praying with Scripture.** We will look at two prayer methods that help us pray with Scripture: Lectio Divina and Imaginative Prayer/Ignatian Contemplation.
- **The Colloquy.** This Ignatian prayer tool invites us to honest, intimate conversations with Mary, Jesus, and God.

- **Principles of Discernment.** St. Ignatius is known for his legacy
  of discernment wisdom. We will look at various discernment
  principles and how they help us know and respond to God's
  invitations.

The problem isn't that we cannot make time for God but that, often, we don't know how to do that. I believe we cannot delay our relationship with God to a later stage of life. From my experience of praying the Ignatian way in my own life and also listening to others' experiences from my position as an Ignatian-trained spiritual director and the twenty-plus years of facilitating Ignatian retreats, I can tell you that every one of us *can* make time for God with the wisdom of Ignatian spirituality to support us. We *can* make time for prayer.

Ignatian spirituality's tools and the promises of God I discovered in my prayer have given me hope and direction—through my young-adult years, the early years of my marriage, and in my season now as a mom. I know now that the source of my hope lies within me, in the inner chapel where God resides. When I go there each day, I spend time with

- Someone who changed my life
- Someone who offers rest, love that is unconditional, and mercy that never runs out
- Someone who offers companionship no matter what I am facing
- Someone who cares enough to come after me, even when I turn away
- Someone who is not afraid to encourage me or even challenge me when I mess up
- Someone who helps me understand the unique gifts and callings of my life.
- Someone who offers me hope, who is the source of my hope

- Someone who shows me that my life has meaning and that I have the capacity for joy

I write this book not from an academic perspective but from that of a layperson who leans on the gifts of Ignatian spirituality every day. While I have twenty years of ministry experience and a master's degree or two, most of what I can share comes from my personal relationship with God and the profound gift of witnessing God at work in other people's lives. I invite you to walk this path too, using the gifts of Ignatian spirituality. As we walk it, we join the millions of others who are on the larger path of Christian faith. Remember that the Ignatian way is simply one spirituality that offers us a way to get to know God. For me it has been the path that led me to understanding and experiencing the inner chapel, where I discovered the promises of God.

LET'S GO TO THE INNER CHAPEL

Praying with Scripture is the basis of St. Ignatius's *Spiritual Exercises.* Scripture plays a huge role in discovering the promises of God. As we pray with Scripture, the ancient words become ever new. In the Spiritual Exercises, we are invited to pray with Scripture and not study it. Praying with Scripture invites us to get to know who God is and the way God works. In a particular way, it helps us get to know Jesus. There are two primary prayer methods offered in the *Spiritual Exercises* to pray with Scripture: meditation and contemplation.

Meditation is reading Scripture and praying over words, ideas, and images. Contemplation invites reading Scripture to move from thinking to feeling and engages our imaginations. We will look at contemplation later in more detail. For now, I want us to focus on meditating on Scripture through a prayer method called Lectio Divina.

Lectio Divina is a slow, rhythmic reading and praying of a Scripture passage. Here are the steps of Lectio Divina:

Before beginning prayer, select a Scripture passage to pray with and have it open in your lap. Begin prayer by settling in and getting quiet. Close your eyes and enter your inner chapel. Invite the Holy Spirit to guide your prayer time.

Read. Pick any passage in Scripture. Slowly, thoughtfully, savor the living word. Linger whenever a word or phrase touches your heart. As you hold the word or phrase that caught your attention, ask yourself, *What might God be offering me?*

Reflect. Read the passage in Scripture a second time. This time, notice what feelings are stirring in response to the reading. Ask yourself, *What is God saying to me in this passage? What is God offering me? Asking me?*

Respond. Read the passage a third time. As the words enter your heart, note which word, image, or idea God is inviting you to savor. Respond to God from your heart. Speak to God of your feelings and insights. Offer these to God.

Rest. You might read the passage a fourth time. As you savor the gift of God's words, simply close your eyes and listen. Sit quietly in God's presence. Rest in God's love. Listen to God in your inner chapel.

I invite you to try the prayer method Lectio Divina with one or more of the Scriptures listed below.

Embracing the Promises of God

These Scriptures can encourage you as you read and pray with them.

- 2 Samuel 7:1–16 // "Do all that you have in mind; for the LORD is with you."
- 2 Corinthians 9:6–15 // "God is able to provide you with every blessing in abundance."
- Luke 15:1–10 // Parables of the lost sheep and lost coin

6

The Importance of
Longing—Ours and God's

St. Mother Teresa said that all humans "long to love and be loved."
We each long to be in relationship, to be known, and to know someone intimately. We long to know that we are not alone. Our human
longings are what send us searching for God in the first place. Over
the years, I have come to discover that my longings and the longings
I notice in others simply need to be directed to God. We are longing
for God, but God is also longing for us. *The very things we long for,*
God longs to give us.

We experience God at work in our lives through the longings we
feel. Sometimes it feels like restlessness. Sometimes it feels like something is off in our lives. Sometimes it is when we find ourselves searching for more and we cannot quite put our finger on what it is we are
searching for. When we feel this longing, though, I want you to rest
assured of something: The longing we feel is God with us. It is one of
the ways God is reminding us that we are not alone, that God is with
us, drawing us ever closer into relationship.

In the Catholic Church, our catechism describing our beliefs
begins with this very teaching.

God, infinitely perfect and blessed in himself, in a plan of sheer goodness freely created man to make him share in his own blessed life. For this reason, at every time and in every place, God draws close to man. He calls man to seek him, to know him, to love him with all his strength. (CCC #1)

This teaching captures that God created humans to share in life with God. In this we see not only that we are made to seek God but also that God desires to draw close to us. God calls us to seek God, to know God, and to love God with all our strength. The way God calls us into relationship is by awakening in us longing or restlessness.

When you notice this feeling, I invite you to wake up to the gift that you are not alone and that God is with you in that moment, longing to be in relationship with you. As St. Augustine says, "Our hearts are restless until they rest in You." Or, as Psalm 62 says, "In God alone is my soul at rest." Our restlessness is a longing for God and God longing for us. It is God's deep desire for intimacy with us, to know and be known by the beloved and share life together.

When we try to satiate this restlessness with someone or something other than God, our longing will never be satisfied. Our deepest human desires to be known fully and to know someone intimately lead us into relationship with God.

Gift of the Holy Spirit

One of St. Ignatius's gifts to us today is his wisdom about discernment. What Ignatius first noticed while lying in bed recovering from a severe war injury was the way God through the Holy Spirit guides us, leading us to discern why we feel longing in the first place. Let me tell you a bit of Ignatius's story to illustrate what I mean.

St. Ignatius was born in Spain and grew up in a wealthy family. He was a soldier and a well-known womanizer. In a battle in Pamplona, Spain, he was struck in the leg by a cannonball and severely injured. He recovered at his family's castle. He was an avid reader, used to reading chivalrous romances. During his recovery, he asked for books to pass the time in bed. There were not books in the castle that he was used to reading. Only two books were available: a book on the life of Christ and one on the lives of the saints.

When he read these two books, he noticed something happening within his heart. There was a longing awakened, a longing to follow in the footsteps of the saints. As he thought about the lives of the saints and following Christ, he noticed within him a change. His heart seemed lighter. He was happy and joyful. What Ignatius noticed over time was that when he dreamed of imitating the saints, his peace and joy stayed for a long time. When he pondered returning to the worldly ways he lived prior to his injury, he felt delight for a short while, but it quickly dissipated and left him feeling dry and unhappy. Over time, Ignatius realized that these were holy desires being awakened within him to imitate the life of the saints and follow Christ. His desires were affirmed by God in prayer when he had a vision of Mary that brought him joy and peace for a long time. From that moment on, God became the focal point of Ignatius's life. He turned completely away from the path of wealth, womanizing, and battle. Ignatius acknowledged that the longing within him was his longing for God and also God's longing for him. As it says in his autobiography, "The result of all this was that he felt within himself a strong impulse to serve our Lord."[3]

We now know that what St. Ignatius experienced during his recovery time was the beginning of the "discernment of spirits." It all began because of his long convalescence, which allowed him time to read and to ponder, to think, and to pray. Ignatius in a sense was

---

3. Joseph Tylenda, *A Pilgrim's Journey: The Autobiography of Ignatius of Loyola* (San Francisco: Ignatius Press, 2001), 51.

going to his inner chapel and paying attention to his longing for God—and God's longing for him.

The same is true for us. Just as the Holy Spirit awakened a longing within Ignatius to follow Christ, which God confirmed by giving Ignatius peace, our longings, too, are awakened and confirmed. Thanks to Ignatius, we now have five-hundred-year-old wisdom to lean on to help us notice God at work in our lives.

St. Ignatius offers us many rules for discernment. I want us to look now at two rules that can teach us to pay attention when we feel longing or restlessness. We can discern if it's the Holy Spirit encouraging us to begin or continue our relationship with God or if it's the evil spirit trying to thwart our growth in our relationship with God. Ultimately, we are looking for what will bring the lasting peace that Ignatius felt when he chose to leave his old ways behind, to engage in a relationship with God, and to let God be the focal point of his life. Here are the contemporary words of the first two rules of discernment from *Draw Me into Your Friendship*, David Fleming's version of the *Spiritual Exercises*.

> When we are caught up in a life of sin or perhaps even if we are closed off from God in one area of our life, the evil spirit is ordinarily accustomed to propose a slothful complacency in the status quo or to entice to a future of ever greater pleasures still to be grasped. The evil one fills our imagination with all kinds of sensual delights and comforts so that there is no will or desire to change the evil direction of our life. The good spirit (the Holy Spirit) uses just the opposite method with us. The good spirit will try to make us see the absurdity of the direction our life has taken. Little by little an uneasiness described sometimes as a "sting" of conscience comes about and a feeling of remorse sets in which stimulates a change from the evil way. (SE #314)

> When we are intent upon living a good life and seeking to pursue the lead of God in our life, the tactics of the spirits are just the

opposite of those described above. The evil spirit proposes to us all the problems and difficulties of living a good life. The evil one attempts to rouse a false sadness for things which will be missed, to instigate anxiety about persevering when we are so weak, and to suggest innumerable roadblocks in walking the way of the Lord. And so the evil spirit tries discouragement and deception to deter us from growing in the Christ-life. The good spirit, however, strengthens and encourages, consoles and inspires, establishes a peace and sometimes moves to a firm resolve. To lead a good life gives delight and joy, and no obstacle seems to be so formidable that it cannot be faced and overcome with God's grace. (SE #315)

What these two rules from the *Spiritual Exercises* help us pay attention to is our longings. There are many things we long for and end up seeking. What Ignatius invites us to pay attention to with his rules of discernment is that if we do not point our longings toward a relationship with God, we will quickly return to a state of restlessness, dryness, and unhappiness.

When we feel longing or restlessness, God is getting our attention about something! The question is, What is it? Is the restlessness we feel the Holy Spirit making us feel remorseful or waking us up to sinful choices that do not lead us to a relationship with God? Or is it the evil spirit's attempt to offer short-lived delights in order to stump us or keep us from continuing on the path of making God our focal point? Throughout the book, I will offer different ways we can experience our longing for God and God's longing for us. The first is noticing the longing that comes from the gift of God's pursuit of us to enter a lifelong relationship with God.

The Goal of Our Life

I hear great angst while listening to people share about how concerned they are that they might not know or discover the goal or purpose for their lives. We often search aimlessly and with a passionate energy seeking to fulfill the *more* we are longing for. I want to invite us to reflect on the opening part of St. Ignatius's First Principle and Foundation, which is found in his *Spiritual Exercises,* to remind us of life's chief goal. I will include the whole text of David Fleming's contemporary translation here, but we will focus only on the first three lines now. We will return to the remaining parts of the First Principle and Foundation later in the book.

The goal of our life is to live with God forever.
God, who loves us, gave us life.
Our own response of love allows God's life to flow into us
    without limit.

All the things in this world are gifts from God,
presented to us so that we can know God more easily
and make a return of love more readily.
As a result, we appreciate and use all these gifts of God
insofar as they help us develop as loving persons.
But if any of these gifts become the center of our lives,
they displace God and so hinder our growth toward our goal.

In everyday life, then, we must hold ourselves in balance
before all of these created gifts insofar as we have a choice
and are not bound by some obligation.
We should not fix our desires on health or sickness,
wealth or poverty, success or failure, a long life or a short one.
For everything has the potential of calling forth in us
a deeper response to our life in God.

Our only desire and our one choice should be this:
I want and I choose what better
leads to God's deepening his life in me.[4]

---

4. David L. Fleming, SJ, *Draw Me into Your Friendship: A Literal Translation and a Contemporary Reading of the Spiritual Exercises* (Boston: Institute of Jesuit Sources, 1996), 27, adapted.

Let's look at the first three lines. They clearly state that the goal of our life is "to live with God forever." What's beautiful about naming this as our goal is also remembering that we are designed to desire this goal. God made us in such a way that we cannot help but seek our goal, which is to live with God forever. Living with God forever does not mean in some far-off time; forever means both now and in our walk to eternal life.

When we find ourselves longing for more, searching and seeking, it is often God awakening us to God's longing for a relationship with *us*. As the next line of the First Principle and Foundation states, "God, who loves us, gave us life." So, the one we long for loves us and created us—and the one who longs for us loves us and created us.

The gnawing sensation we feel might be God getting our attention about spending time with God. This type of longing or restlessness might show up when

- we are starting our relationship with God for the first time.
- we are re-beginning a relationship with God after being away from it for a while.
- we are being drawn into a deeper level of relationship with God.

I most often hear this longing described as "something is missing from my life" or "I am looking for more." I grin when I hear people name this type of longing because I am profoundly witnessing God's pursuit of them. I even chuckle sometimes and say, "That's God coming after you!"

The *something* missing in our lives is often not a *what* but a *who*. The search for *more* is not a new item on our task list or an added responsibility but a relationship with God. The Holy Spirit moves within us and raises desires in our hearts to fulfill those longings for a relationship that fills all things, that offers unconditional love, and that provides meaning to our lives.

What, then, is our response when we feel this type of restlessness or longing? We can turn to the third line of the First Principle and Foundation: "Our own response of love allows God's life to flow into us without limit." Our response to this longing is one of love when we acknowledge that it is happening and we pause to see what God might be inviting us to tend to.

When we feel this type of longing, we can ask,

- Do I have a relationship with God? Is God inviting me into a relationship?
- How is my relationship with God? Is God inviting me to return to God?
- How might God be inviting me to grow deeper in our relationship?

When we feel this type of longing or restlessness, it is God's desire for a relationship with us, and a remedy is simply to start spending time with God. Through this time together in our inner chapel, God helps us move God to the center of our lives. This doesn't happen overnight or in one fell swoop but over time. And what is deeply comforting to me is, as much as we are longing for God, God is also longing for us. Let's take a look at that now.

God Longs for Us

Here's the question: Do we believe that, in the middle of all the busyness we are facing and what is happening today, God longs for us? That God not only longs for us but is already here with us?

A cherished memory from my childhood was the annual Christmas Eve candlelight service at my dad's side of the family's Methodist church. Every year, my large family of many Christian denominations gathered there first before our family Christmas party. It was one of the rare occasions during the year when we would all be at church together. We would fill multiple rows, and all the cousins would scramble to sit next to one another during the service. We came dressed in our Christmas best, eyes glowing in full anticipation of the joy-filled evening ahead. For me as a young child, the service droned on forever, only delaying the moment we could enjoy my aunt's sugar cookies and the exchange of presents.

During my high school years, though, the ritual of gathering at the candlelight service took on a different meaning. The ritual of beginning our family Christmas celebration with the candlelight service year after year spoke profoundly to me about the importance and value of faith. The witness of what my grandparents, parents, aunts, and uncles held as the priority on Christmas Eve influenced me through college and into my adult years. Many years later as a parent of three, I seek to pass this on to my own children. I hope that they experience what I did in the rituals and traditions of my family's faith that were part of my childhood.

I hope that they understand the powerful meaning of the words of the song we sang at my grandparents' church every year on Christmas Eve: "Emmanuel, Emmanuel. His name is called Emmanuel. God with us, revealed in us. His name is called Emmanuel" (Bob McGee). As I sang those words every Christmas Eve with my large extended family, I knew in my bones that God *was* with us and that God *was* in each of us. That is the legacy I hope to pass on to my children—the understanding that God resides within them. This is the fuel for my ministry work and call as well: to help people like you understand that God resides in each of us and is still Emmanuel—God with us.

I think of the many examples in the Gospels where people feel alone or longing or restless in some way, seeking some sort of hope that they are not alone and that there is hope for them. What strikes me when I read the Gospels is that when these people finally point their longing to Jesus, he is already there to meet them. Think about Zacchaeus (Luke 19:1–10), who scrambles up the tree to get a glimpse at Jesus passing by. Jesus sees him and notices his longing for him and stops, looks him in the eye, and says, "Zacchaeus, hurry and come down; for I must stay at your house today." There was no chance for Zacchaeus to run home and tidy up and get things in order before Jesus entered his house. Jesus met him immediately in his longing. Or think about the woman at the well who is thirsting and longing for the Messiah (John 4:4–42). Jesus meets her at the well and tells her, "I am he." What she is longing for is literally right in front of her! What we are longing for is right in front of us. The fountain of living water that stems from a relationship with God is right in front of us. God is already there waiting for us to acknowledge God's presence within us and in daily life.

God is longing for us. Longing to be in relationship with us. To offer us the very intimacy we seek even with our dark parts, our sin, aspects of our lives that are not all in order. God longs to be in relationship with us because God created us and loves us. Not only does God long to be in relationship with us, but God also longs to offer us the living water that Jesus offered the woman at the well. The living waters of love, mercy, and forgiveness. Living waters that console us, heal us, strengthen us, lift us up, unbind us, and set us free. God longs to bring us along a path that offers peace the world cannot give.

Do you see God longing for you? Do you believe God is right here in front of you, inviting you, welcoming you into a relationship?

LET'S GO TO THE INNER CHAPEL

Pause a moment and go to your inner chapel. Notice any longings within you.

- Do you find yourself searching and seeking for more?
- Do you find yourself restless at all, feeling as if nothing will satisfy you?
- Do you feel yourself drawn in inexplicable ways towards God?

Jot down anything that occurs to you or any emotion that arises. How do you feel your longings at work? What do you sense of God's longing for you? How does it make you feel to know God is longing for a relationship with you? What might be your next steps to respond to the longings within you?

Embracing the Promises of God

These Scriptures can encourage you as you read them and pray with them.

- Sirach 2:1–11 // "Trust in [God], and he will help you; make your ways straight, and hope in him. Wait for his mercy; . . . trust him. . . . Hope for good things, for lasting joy and mercy. . . . The Lord is compassionate and merciful; he forgives sins and saves in time of distress."
- Psalm 42 // "As a deer longs for flowing streams, / so my soul longs for you, O God."
- Hebrews 11:1–7 // "And without faith it is impossible to please God, for whoever would approach him must believe that he exists and that he rewards those who seek him."
- John 10:1–10 // "I came that [you] may have life, and have it abundantly."

PART 2

EMBRACING THE PROMISES OF GOD

7

Jesus Invites Us into Relationship

On a sunny afternoon, I watched Boppy breathe as he quietly slept in his hospice bed on their sunporch. His inhales and exhales served as a grounding rhythm that steadied me even in the uncertainty we faced in week six of hospice care. As I sat next to Boppy's bed watching each inhale and exhale, the mix of emotions was familiar. I was reminded of the hours I stood over my children's cribs when they first came home from the hospital. The immediate depth of love I felt for these tiny human beings always surprised me, and watching them breathe during the night or a nap often stirred a strong mix of emotions: love that felt as if it would burst out of my chest, a fierce instinct to protect them, and the fear of losing them. I can remember moments when my love for them was so profound that with each inhale they took I feared the exhale would not follow. It was as if each release of tiny breath brought relief that my child was still there. I felt that same relief as I watched Boppy's chest rise and fall. I became tearful as I thought of what life would be without him. It was hard to imagine what it would be like to not have his companionship through all of life's little moments, not to mention the big ones.

Knowing that it was time for me to head home to meet the kids after school, I prepared to tell him goodbye for the day. I paused to savor the gift of our relationship before leaning in to kiss his bald head goodbye, gently, trying not to wake him. As I pulled back, I felt his hand grab my arm, and then his eyes opened. "Oh, good, you are here. I have some things I want to talk to you about." I sat back down beside him, readying myself to take mental notes of the many details he was concerned about being forgotten, details ensuring my grandmother would be taken care of. This afternoon, though, he had other things on his mind.

He asked me, "Becksa, are you going to write another book?" I told him I was thinking about it, and he asked me what I was thinking of writing about. I shared my ideas of a few themes I was pondering: hope, discernment, prayer life. He closed his eyes and listened, gently nodding his head in agreement. A few tears rolled out of the corners of his eyes before he opened them and spoke. "I can't imagine life without Jesus. Can you?" I agreed. He continued, "I am thankful I am not alone in this world, and I never have been. I am thankful that Jesus is here with me right now. I am thankful for his companionship and love throughout my life." Then, looking at me with his bright blue eyes, he said, "Promise me you will not stop doing what you are doing. Promise me you will continue to spread the Good News to others. Promise me you will tell people what we understand about the gift of a relationship with Jesus."

In some ways, this is the hardest chapter for me to put into words. How do I describe a relationship that is as real to me as my relationship with my grandfather was—even though I have never met Jesus in the flesh? How do I share the strength that Jesus' companionship gives me without showing you the physical person? How do I describe this person I have come to know and understand through the years of going to my inner chapel to spend time with him? How do I put into words that our humanity is reflected and understood in Jesus and that he gets what we go through? How do I describe that he is the source of our ability to have faith, hope, and love?

The Life-Changing Relationship

Getting to know Jesus changed my life. My relationship with Jesus still changes me as I am drawn ever deeper into the waters of intimacy with him. The Good News I so desperately and urgently want to share with each of you is that this relationship is available to you. Not only is it available, but Jesus is already inviting you into it. It's like the ocean image from an earlier chapter: Jesus is standing on the shore next to us long before we realize it, inviting us into the waters of relationship with him.

Jesus calls each of us into relationship, just as he called the first disciples. His invitation to them was, "Follow me, and I will make you fish for people." They dropped their nets and followed him (Matthew 4:18–22; Mark 1:16–20; Luke 5:11). As they began their relationship with Jesus and walked with him, they learned who he was, how he loved, and how to follow him in their daily lives. The same is true for each of us. We are invited to get to know Jesus intimately so, as stated in the *Spiritual Exercises* of St. Ignatius, we can have "interior knowledge of the Lord . . . so that we might love Him and follow him more closely" (SE #104).

While I do not know the exact time, at some point Jesus called my grandfather into relationship, invited Boppy to follow him, just as Jesus called me into relationship with him during my junior year of high school and invited me to follow him. One of the most beautiful things to witness in the ministry of spiritual direction is Jesus inviting people into a relationship and then watching the ways Jesus calls people deeper, revealing to them more and more about himself along the way.

Jesus is inviting *you* into a personal relationship with him. This invitation lasts our whole lives and goes beyond our initial "net-dropping" moment when we choose to follow him. Jesus invites us every moment to know and experience his companionship and friendship. Before we go any further, though, let's pause and reflect on our net-dropping moment.

Net-Dropping Moment

I took a long sip of hot coffee to give me a minute to process the question. Sitting across from me was a man in his late twenties who had just asked me, "When did you first encounter Jesus?" Not only was I thrown off by the depth of his question, asked within minutes of our meeting each other, but I was also not prepared to be the one asked this type of question. When he asked to meet, I assumed that *I* would be in the role of spiritual director, offering questions to help him reflect on his own faith journey!

It had been a long time since I'd reflected on the beginning of my faith journey—those early moments when I felt Jesus calling me into relationship, inviting me to drop my nets and follow him. The moments when my eyes were opened and my heart burned within me as the disciples' hearts did on the road to Emmaus. The moments when I was drawn inexplicably to Jesus by a restlessness and desire to learn more. The moments when I was almost giddy with joy as I became aware of Jesus' presence in my life.

I saw in the young man the same inquisitive nature that I possess—the part of me that loves to hear people's faith stories and the part of me that loves to hear about when Jesus got people's attention. I could feel his question hitting me in a deep place; it was a nudge from God to remember where it all began. I did my best to share my beginnings of encountering Jesus, and then I eagerly listened to the young man's story. It invigorated me tremendously both to share my own story and to hear his. Listening to his story and sharing mine reminded me of Fr. Pedro Arrupe's words.

Nothing is more practical than
finding God, than
falling in Love
in a quite absolute, final way.
What you are in love with,
what seizes your imagination, will affect everything.
It will decide
what will get you out of bed in the morning,
what you do with your evenings,
how you spend your weekends,
what you read, whom you know,
what breaks your heart,
and what amazes you with joy and gratitude.
Fall in Love, stay in love,
and it will decide everything.[5]

The young man and I both had experiences of falling in love with God through a relationship with Jesus, and it changed everything. It changed what we did with our time, what motivated us, what set our hearts on fire, and how we lived day to day.

I wonder what your initial encounter with Jesus was? Maybe you are in the middle of an initial net-dropping moment right now. Maybe your call to enter a relationship with Jesus came years ago. Maybe there is a deeper invitation from Jesus to drop everything and follow him even more closely. The invitation continues throughout our lives to embrace the gift of friendship with Jesus and to get to know him in a tangible, personal way. The promises of God help us to open up and become free to follow Jesus. We are invited to come

---

5. Jim Manney, *God Finds Us: An Experience of the Spiritual Exercises of St. Ignatius Loyola* (Chicago: Loyola Press, 2013), 17.

and see, to follow Jesus, and to leave our nets behind. As we do, our lives will transform. Here's a little story to illustrate what I mean.

Rebuild Me to Shelter Your Name

The prayer slipped out of my lips without much thought: "Rebuild me to shelter your name." The phrase was inspired by a song by Danielle Rose called "Shelter Your Name" that I had played on repeat over the last several months.

The second I spoke these words years ago, I wanted to take them back. What in the world did I just ask for? Transformation? Rebuilding? Change? What was I thinking?!

The words I prayed brought together my outward life with what I had discovered in my inner chapel. In the years since my net-dropping moments in high school and college, when I began to intentionally nurture my relationship with God through prayer, I had developed a personal relationship with Jesus. This relationship awakened me to an understanding of God's love and mercy, to the fact that I was not alone, that I belonged to someone, and that Jesus fully revealed God to me.

As the gifts of this relationship with Jesus developed, I felt a growing desire for my insides to match my outsides, which led me to this moment of prayer, asking God to "rebuild me to shelter your name." I longed to shelter all that I understood within my inner chapel but also in the exterior of my life. This desire led to a transformation from the inside out. I was beginning to understand that a relationship with Jesus was not just about me and him but also about carrying out to others what I learned in my inner chapel.

The interior knowledge of the Lord that I had was about the ability to follow Jesus more closely, and in the school of prayer I realized that getting to know Jesus meant a complete transformation of my life, both internally and externally. It was as if I were being invited to live as a mirror that received immense light and love from Jesus, and as it poured into me, I was being invited to reflect it back to the world around me.

Being rebuilt to shelter Jesus' name was a transforming process. Honestly, that process is still happening. It reminds me of a quote by St. Ignatius: "There are very few people who realize what God would make of them if they abandoned themselves into his hands, and let themselves be formed by his grace."

When I prayed those words, "Rebuild me to shelter your name," I had no idea what might be in store for me. Fortunately, we are given a very clear model in Jesus of what it means to shelter God's name. Our inner chapels are our shelter for what it means to follow Jesus.

Getting to Know the One Who Calls Us

A grace we are suggested to pray for in the *Spiritual Exercises* of St. Ignatius is that God help us get to know Jesus more intimately, to love him more intensely, and to follow Jesus more closely. Ultimately, what this means is becoming more like Jesus by learning to see like Jesus, hear like Jesus, love like Jesus, and act like Jesus. It means not only hearing the call to follow Jesus but also to walk with him and be there working with him. As we get to know him and to love him, we learn to follow his way and live the model he lays out for us.

Getting to know Jesus helps us understand God. Jesus' words in the Gospel of John state clearly that Jesus reveals God to us when he says, "I am the way, and the truth, and the life. No one comes to the Father except through me. If you know me, you will know my Father also" (John 14:6–7). Over the years of going to my inner chapel and praying with Scripture, I got to know Jesus, and getting to know Jesus helped me get to know God and the Holy Spirit as well. Ultimately, Jesus helped me discover the promises of God. Jesus made visible what was invisible, as we are reminded in Colossians 1:15. While Jesus is no longer walking around on earth today, through our praying with Jesus' life in Scripture, Jesus is made real and personal to us and makes God, who is invisible, visible to us.

St. John Paul II reminds us that

> the vital core of the new evangelization must be a clear and unequivocal proclamation of the person of Jesus Christ, that is, the preaching of his name, his teaching, his life, his promises and the Kingdom, which he has gained for us by his Paschal Mystery.[6]

Learning to follow Jesus begins with getting to know the one who calls us into relationship. The way we do this is by contemplating the life of Christ. We do this through praying with the Gospels that reveal the many aspects of Jesus' life. Fr. Kevin O'Brien captures this idea in his book *The Ignatian Adventure.*

> When contemplating the Gospels, we are often gifted with memories from our lives that correspond to Jesus' life. These memories can be gifts because through our prayerful remembering, past hurts may be healed. Or we may appreciate how God has been at work in unexpected ways or previously overlooked ways. Or we may gain some insight into significant events in our history.[7]

The way we contemplate the mysteries of Jesus' life is through praying with Scripture—by using Lectio Divina, which we discussed in chapter 5, or imaginative prayer, which we will discuss at the end of this chapter.

As we pray with the Gospels of Jesus' life, we can reflect on these questions.

---

6. John Paul II, apostolic exhortation *Ecclesia in America* (Rome: Libreria Editrice Vaticana, 1999).

7. Kevin O'Brien, SJ, *The Ignatian Adventure: Experiencing the Spiritual Exercises of St. Ignatius in Daily Life* (Chicago: Loyola Press, 2011), 147.

- What memories from my life correspond to Jesus' life?
- What memories from my past were healed through following Jesus' life?
- How did I discover God at work in my own life through remembering Jesus' life?
- What new insights did I gain through the significant events of my life and Jesus' life?
- Jesus revealed God fully—all the promises are revealed in him. How am I revealing God to others?

Understanding Jesus' Humanity

Praying with the life of Jesus helps us understand Jesus' humanity. The way I really came to understand Jesus' humanity was when I was making the Spiritual Exercises and praying with the Scriptures of Jesus' childhood. At the time, Brady, our son, was two and a half years old, and our daughter Abby was six months old. My days at that moment were consumed with caring for an infant and a toddler, which meant that most of my days revolved around tending to the basic needs of feeding children, of helping them with bathroom needs, and of rocking them to sleep. As I prayed with the Scripture of Jesus being born and Mary pondering things in her heart, I connected deeply with her as a mother. I understood that she once tended to Jesus' same needs to eat, to sleep, and to go to the bathroom. I do not share this to be disrespectful to Jesus but simply to share how the Gospels became real to me through connecting them to what was going on in my life. At the time, it was tending to young children the way Mary tended to her son, Jesus.

At later times in life, I understood different aspects of Jesus' humanity based on what was going on in my life. The living Word of God became real and alive to me as I saw Jesus experiencing uncertainty of his call and Mary encouraging him to step forth at the wedding of Cana, or Jesus at his baptism being affirmed of God's love for him, as I need that affirmation as well. I saw, too, that Jesus lived in community and had close friends and experienced all the human realities of what relationships can bring at times: joy, love, hope, and even betrayal, abandonment, and hurt.

Jesus also taught me the value of going to my inner chapel every day. His model of prayer was one I felt compelled to replicate. When I saw him praying at various times of day, it encouraged me to make time to go to my inner chapel. His communal aspect of faith encourages me to make Mass and the sacraments regular parts of my life.

It brought me great courage to watch Jesus' prayer being interrupted by the crowds when one of my children would wake up early and interrupt my prayer time. Jesus' example still encourages me to continue with my prayer when life's rhythms or responsibilities make it a little more difficult to keep up with my prayer routine. I drew strength from Jesus' model of this especially during the time of caring for my grandfather and juggling my other responsibilities. The prayer by his hospital bed or in the waiting room surrounded by the noise of the hospital was as meaningful as prayer in my sacred space at home in the quiet morning in my chair, coffee in hand, before the rest of my house woke up.

Jesus continued in both his prayer and his ministry. He allowed the beautiful tension between quiet time in his inner chapel with God and the interrupted prayers when he had to tend to the needs of the people around him. I receive great strength from the witness of his life and better understand how I can replicate it in my own life.

Contemplating the way Jesus healed people has a profound impact on me. As I watch Jesus heal people such as the man with the withered hand, the hemorrhaging woman, the paralyzed man on the mat, the crippled woman, and so many more, it reminds me that the same power available to them to be healed is available to us. It is through our connection with Jesus—our time with him in the inner chapel—that his power moves from him to us. When we go to our inner chapel, we encounter Jesus the same way Jesus encountered people tangibly when he was walking around on earth.

So, imagine each day encountering Jesus in a personal way in your inner chapel—over and over again receiving the gift of his love, his mercy, and his friendship. This is how we are transformed—by going to our inner chapels every day and letting the healing power of Jesus into our hearts. Eventually, that power permeates our lives and is passed along to those who need it.

St. Ignatius shares a beautiful image of water dropping into a sponge versus water dropping onto a stone (SE #335). When we are making progress in the spiritual life, he says that the Holy Spirit feels like a drop of water that gently soaks into a sponge versus the evil spirit feeling like water hitting a stone. I believe encountering Jesus in our inner chapel feels like gentle drops of water soaking into a sponge. Over time, as we continue to encounter Jesus, the drops of water saturate the sponge to the point that the sponge can no longer hold the water anymore. The water begins oozing out of the sponge to the surfaces around it. This is how it is with us. Our relationship with Jesus is never just about us; it is about understanding who he is in an experiential, interior way so that we can bring the gifts of this relationship out into the world. It is never only about the love given to us but also about the love we share with others. It's not only about the mercy and healing Jesus gives us but also about sharing this experience of mercy and healing with others.

This is ultimately what the poem from Fr. Arrupe is all about: Falling in love with God changes everything. It changes what gets us out of bed in the morning and how we spend our time throughout the day—throughout the weeks and months and our whole lives. This personal encounter with Jesus changes everything about our lives. It has changed—and keeps changing—mine.

Friendship with Jesus

My life is changed because of a friendship with Jesus. My grandfather's life was also. This gift of companionship is what Boppy and I talked about not only that day on his sunporch but also in the wee hours of many nights in his hospital room after surgeries and many other moments over the years. We both knew that Jesus is alive and relevant in our current time and in daily life. Boppy understood that this gift of friendship with Jesus was not only there for him through the good times but also there in times of suffering and especially as he faced the end of earthly life.

This gift of friendship with Jesus is available to every one of us. He is inviting us, calling us into relationship. As we say yes to this relationship and begin following his way, we discover and embrace the promises of God that Jesus reveals to us.

LET'S GO TO THE INNER CHAPEL

Ignatian Contemplation

As I mentioned in chapter 5, praying with Scripture is the basis of St. Ignatius's *Spiritual Exercises*. There are two primary prayer methods offered in the *Spiritual Exercises* to pray with Scripture: meditation and contemplation. We already focused on meditation using the prayer tool Lectio Divina. Now I would like us to turn to Ignatian contemplation, or what is sometimes called imaginative prayer. While meditation focuses on the words and phrases of the Scripture, Ignatian contemplation focuses on our feelings and engages our imaginations and our senses.

Ignatian contemplation is a prayer method St. Ignatius recommends when praying with the life of Jesus. It not only allows us to hear and read the words of Jesus but also moves what is going on in the Scripture into our imaginations. This helps us not only hear Jesus but also watch the way he moves and acts.

Here are the steps of Ignatian contemplation, or imaginative prayer.

1. **Select a Scripture.** Pick a passage from one of the four Gospels: Matthew, Mark, Luke, or John.

2. **Read.** Read the passage several times slowly so that you almost know the story well enough to share with another person.

3. **Imagine the scene.** Close your eyes and imagine the scene. Imagine what the scene looks like. Who is in the scene? What are they doing? Where are they located? What do you notice about the environment? What smells are there? What sounds? Let the Holy Spirit guide this unfolding in your mind for you.

4. **Put yourself in the scene.** As the scene begins to take shape in your mind, put yourself in the scene. Notice where you are.

5. **Notice what happens.** Let the story unfold in your mind. Stay with it until you feel nudged to move to reflection.

6. **Respond and rest.** Share with God what you noticed and experienced. Then rest in God and let God speak to you.

7. **Reflect.** Reflect on what you experienced in prayer. What did you learn about Jesus? About God? About another character in the Scripture? About yourself?

Embracing the Promises of God

These Scriptures can encourage you as you read them and pray with them.

As we seek to get to the One who calls, what aspects of Jesus' life are you being invited to get to know more? Read through the list of suggested Scriptures and mark a few that you feel drawn to. Over the next few days, try using Ignatian contemplation to pray with the Scriptures you marked. Contemplate Jesus' life and make note of what Jesus is teaching you about yourself, himself, the Holy Spirit, God.

- Luke 19:1–10 // Jesus calls Zacchaeus.
- John 15:15 // "I have called you friends, because I have made known to you everything that I have heard from my Father."
- John 14:6 // "I am the way, the truth, and the life."
- John 13.15 // "I have set you an example that you also should do as I have done to you."
- Luke 6:6–11 // Jesus cures the man with the withered hand.
- John 4:1–14 // "Whoever comes to Jesus never thirsts."
- John 10:1–21 // Jesus is the Good Shepherd; he knows my name and he cares for me.
- Luke 5:27–32 // Call of Levi (the sinner)—Jesus calls me, too.
- Mark 9:14–29 // I have faith; help my little faith.
- Luke 15:1–32 // Three parables about God's merciful love
- Luke 13:10–17 // Jesus wants to heal anyone who suffers: healing of a crippled woman on the Sabbath.
- John 1:1–18 // Jesus comes and stays in my humanity.
- Matthew 9:20–22 // Jesus cures the hemorrhaging woman.

8

There Is Rest for the Weary

Weariness comes in all shapes and sizes. Sometimes it comes from burning the candle at both ends. Other times it stems from carrying a heavy load for a long time. Weariness comes from holding on to a job, a relationship, or even a call from God long after we were invited to let it go. It can hit us after an intense season that required more effort and a more rapid pace than are normal for us. The weight of our tiredness can overwhelm and surprise us when we finally notice it. The exhaustion can go far beyond just the physical and can also become weariness of mind and spirit. Thank goodness God promises us rest! Going to the inner chapel provides rest.

A woman I met with in spiritual direction walked in my door one day with a tiredness in her eyes that has become all too familiar for many of us these days. Her eyes were *tired*. I could sense how the weight and weariness of life had caught up with her as she had attempted to work and raise her four children. During our spiritual direction session, something began to gnaw at me, but I couldn't really identify it. When our session was over, I sat at my desk and began to think through the past week's interactions with people in spiritual direction, on retreats, and in my daily life with friends, family, and fellow parents. I listed the conversations I'd had with people that echoed the themes of my worn-out directee. Then I counted what I had listed: Twenty conversations during that week had contained themes of tiredness, weariness, exhaustion, and struggling to keep up! I also knew that conversations not on that list included the ones between my husband and me—and they had echoed those same themes. I remembered times we both asked, *Why are the days so full? Why are there so many meetings? Why do we feel we can never get caught up on e-mails?* I pondered the moments that week that spoke to these themes, such as when Chris and I high-fived each other after getting a text that a kids' practice was canceled due to inclement weather or when we texted each other with "Woohoo! Meeting just got canceled!"

My mind raced to books and articles I've read about the impact busyness has on our bodies, our ability to focus, our productivity, and our creativity. I pondered the research I'd heard at recent ministry conferences at which we were presented with the changing stats of ministry life. Across the spectrum the messages were the same: We are being asked to do more with fewer people and resources, all while the hunger of people is growing exponentially. I sat, perplexed. As I let all this sink in, I asked aloud, "What the heck is going on here, God?"

While I wish I could tell you God poured out some clear-as-day answer in that moment, I cannot. But what I *can* tell you is that as I sat at my desk that afternoon, I knew that God had brought something significant to my attention that had to do with my calls as a married mother of three and also as a lay minister.

I feel that God was bringing to mind another aspect of the Good News that we need to remember right now: the promise of rest for the weary. I chuckled as I named this because it reminded me of the closing line of the old G.I. Joe cartoons that my brothers used to watch: "Knowing is half the battle." There was a time when I needed rest, but someone else had to recognize that need and point it out to me.

My Thirst for Rest

In the summer of 2013, my husband gave me a silent retreat for my birthday. As Chris explained why he chose this gift for me, I realized that my need for rest was apparently showing up in daily life, around the people I loved. Chris gently shared all the ways he was noticing my tiredness and invited me to "go on this retreat to deeply rest and take care of what is going on within you."

During the past year, we had moved across the country, and Chris knew the transition had been a hard one for all of us, including our children. There were tears and sadness as we maneuvered the move. The past year was the first year of kindergarten for our son. The combination of moving states and entering full-day school proved to be a hard transition for him. My mother heart still aches at the memories of holding my young son in my arms, attempting to comfort his sobs as he longed for familiarity, for friends and community he knew, and for his home. The year had held six months of no work for my husband as the economy tanked and he left grad school and, along with the thousands of others in 2012, went looking for employment.

In the middle of life, I was attempting to meet people for spiritual direction and offer retreats. And just a couple of weeks earlier we had learned the amazing news that I was pregnant with our third child, something we had longed for the past several years. The news helped me understand the physical tiredness that had crept in lately that only seemed to compound my mental weariness.

As I received Chris's words and gift, a mix of emotions arose. I was thankful for the gift, but I also felt some angst and frustration at his honest words that he could notice how tired I was. It made me wonder if others in my life had noticed the signs of tiredness. In the days after my birthday, I took an honest look at myself and realized that there were signs everywhere of how tired I was. Life's pace and the focus on settling our family and children had kept me from paying attention to what was going on. In hindsight, I wished I had stopped and noticed earlier what was happening before I got to the point of total exhaustion. I realized I was teetering on burnout.

I look to these memories often to continue to glean lessons from them. That season of life reminded me of two things: how to notice our own thirst for rest and also how to carve out rest in our day-to-day life. Let's look first at how we notice our own thirst for rest.

Noticing Our Thirst for Rest

St. Ignatius offers many tools from his discernment wisdom to help us notice our thirst for rest. Much of his discernment wisdom is about noticing the movements of consolation and desolation in our lives.

Consolation is an experience of feeling on fire with God's love that impels us to love and serve God and love and serve others. Consolation often inspires gratitude toward God for all God's gifts of love, mercy, friendship, and faithfulness. When we are in consolation, we might feel more alive, more connected to God and to other people. Turning to St. Ignatius's direct words on spiritual consolation, we read:

> Finally, under the word consolation I include every increase in hope, faith, and charity, and every interior joy which calls and attracts one toward heavenly things and to the salvation of one's soul, by bringing it tranquility and peace in its Creator and Lord. (SE #316)[8]

While in consolation we feel increases in hope, faith, love, and a rise in energy for love and service to God and others, in desolation we feel the exact opposite. We might feel a tiredness or heaviness. We might feel disconnected from God and from people. Our energy and

---

8. George E. Ganss, SJ, *The Spiritual Exercises of Saint Ignatius* (Chicago: Loyola Press, 1992), 122.

passion decrease. St. Ignatius offers these words to describe desolation as entirely opposite of consolation.

> By [this kind of] desolation, I mean . . . obtuseness of soul, turmoil within it, an impulsive motion toward low and earthly things, or disquiet from various agitations and temptations. These move one toward lack of faith and leave one without hope and without love. One is completely listless, tepid, and unhappy and feels separated from our Creator and Lord. (SE #317)[9]

St. Ignatius suggests that when we notice signs of desolation, we need to pause and dig into them and notice what the cause might be. Fr. Timothy Gallagher in his presentations on Ignatian discernment speaks about desolation starting out the size of a snowball at the top of a mountain. He says that when our desolation begins, we can stop the snowball with our finger at the top of the mountain. However, if we do not pause and notice it, then the snowball picks up speed, and the small snowball turns into an avalanche.

When I think of all the moments that led up to Chris gifting me with a retreat, I know there were snowball-size signs of desolation that I simply neglected: physical fatigue, struggle to focus, lack of energy about things I'd once had passion for, a heightened sense of agitation, and snippiness. Looking back, I saw desolation that began small, like a snowball, but I did not fully stop to acknowledge it or to do anything about it. So, the snowball of tiredness continued down the mountain and grew and grew until I was out of gas and sputtering in almost every area of my life. This is why I was on the brink of total exhaustion and burnout.

When we leave rest unattended, it impacts all areas of our life, including our bodies. We struggle to sleep, to fall asleep, and to stay asleep. Weariness raises blood pressure and causes inflammation. It

9. Ganss, *Spiritual Exercises*, 122.

can trigger unhealthy changes in diet because we tend to reach for sugar and caffeine when our energy is low. Weariness—whether of body or spirit—will weaken the immune system and dull our reactions, making us vulnerable to illness and injury.

Let's take a look at a few ways we can pause and notice our own thirst for rest. I invite you to go through the checklist and note the ones that apply to you now or have in the past. Once you note those, take a moment to ask yourself what the root cause might be. St. Ignatius invites us to look for the source of desolation.

- Angry
  - *Do I feel I am snapping at people closest to me?*
  - *Am I growing resentful in any way?*
  - *Am I agitated or feel as if I have a short fuse?*
- Anxious
  - *Do I feel restless?*
  - *Do I feel overwhelmed?*
  - *Is worry making it hard to make positive choices and changes?*
- Doubtful
  - *Am I doubting myself?*
  - *Am I questioning my gifts?*
  - *Am I feeling unequipped to respond to my calls?*
- Hungry
  - *Do I find myself physically hungry?*
  - *Do I find myself hungering for more constantly, which is leading me to numb my hunger?*
- Lonely
  - *Do I feel alone?*
  - *Do I feel lonely?*

- *Do I feel isolated or as if I am turning away from the people in my life?*
- *Do I feel as if I am lacking community and support right now?*

• Overwhelmed

- *Am I feeling overwhelmed?*
- *Do I feel stuck and that there is no way out?*

• Tepid

- *Do I lack energy or passion for things I once liked to do?*
- *Do I feel slothful?*

• Tired

- *Am I physically sleepy?*
- *Am I mentally or emotionally weary?*
- *Am I lacking energy for my normal responsibilities?*
- *Am I having trouble sleeping?*

I want to suggest a few reasons for our tiredness that I notice from my own life and from listening to others. Please feel free to add your own.

• We are overcommitted and have too much on our plates.

• We are not tending to our basic human needs of sleep, healthy foods, exercise, and water.

• We are overconnected to technology and not giving our brains a chance to rest and replenish.

• We are neglecting our prayer life and relationship with God.

• We are not honoring our need for community and are neglecting valued relationships such as those with significant others, friends, and family.

• We are in a season of transition or loss and are not giving ourselves the space to grieve.

Once we notice our thirst for rest, it is important for us to remember that God promises us rest for the weary.

Definition and Value of Rest

To begin with, let's look at the definition of rest. One dictionary definition of *rest* is "to cease work or movement in order to relax, refresh oneself, and to recover strength." Considering the busyness and exhaustion we are experiencing, it appears that we have missed key aspects of rest in our day-to-day lives. We so rarely slow down, cease movement, or pause anymore.

As I read the definitions of rest, I grimaced, because they capture what our society and culture have come to believe as truth: we are on our own, even when it comes to providing our own renewal.

But the Good News for us is that we are not completely on our own when it comes to rest. God supports us and helps us by providing invitations for rest and by helping us refresh ourselves and recover our strength. Where do we go for rest, and how can we embrace this promise of God's rest for the weary?

In the Gospel of Matthew, Jesus says, "Come to me, all you that are weary and are carrying heavy burdens, and I will give you rest" (Matthew 11:28–30). Jesus tells us that if we come to him, he will give us rest and lighten our loads. Our part is to come to him, and Jesus, who is our still point, is the source of our rest.

Jesus Is the Still Point

Have you ever taught a child to ride a bike with no training wheels? When our youngest, Mary, was a month shy of turning five, she came and stood before me with her big ole brown eyes and blond hair and, with her hands on her hips, pronounced to me, "Mom, it's time for me to ride with no training wheels. I have to learn before I am five." Not knowing where she got this idea in her mind, I knew better than to try to dissuade my tenacious four-year-old away from this goal of riding a bike the way her older brother and sister ride.

Chris and I removed the training wheels off her pink Disney princess bike and, with full tenacity, Mary jumped on the bike, determined to take off pedaling on her own. As you can imagine, she made it one pedal push before her bike toppled to the side. Not to be discouraged, Mary hopped on again and tried to take off pedaling with no training wheels. Again she quickly fell, this time hurting her knee. Fear entered her at this point as she realized that a life with no training wheels can cause harm. Watching her reminded me of myself once I learned that *life* with no training wheels can hurt sometimes.

Chris and I coaxed her gently back onto her bike with the assurance that we would be there as her guides, holding the seat tightly as she became familiar with how to balance on a bike with no training wheels. Up and down the driveway we went that afternoon. As we did, her confidence grew, but not to the point where she was ready for us to let go. Over the next few days, this became part of our after-school ritual, and we began letting go for short periods of time as she was released from one of her parents' or siblings' hands to pedal a short distance into the hands of another trusted family member. Even with encouragement and practice, Mary was overtaken by fear. She would begin pedaling and start to look backward or to the sides instead of keeping her eyes fixed forward. Every time she did this, her bike became very wobbly, and she went all over the place, often crashing at the end.

After about two weeks of this, my patience was beginning to wear thin on this afternoon activity. So one Sunday afternoon, Chris and I were determined to help her learn this so that her confidence would be okay for a life-long skill, but, honestly, also so we could be done with chasing her. This sunny afternoon, our neighbors gathered outside to cheer Mary on as they had done many afternoons prior. Her little friend across the street busted out poms-poms for this occasion. She and her little brother chanted and cheered as Mary made it farther and farther. Mary's confidence, though, would wane quickly as she was released from one of our hands and her wobbling began again.

We began to encourage her by celebrating every square she made it past on the bike path sidewalk. Her brother and sister cheered her on. Mary, you made it two squares! Now you've made it five squares! Chris and I cheered her on as she went longer and longer distances and as we watched her confidence and skills grow. Sensing she was ready to really go, we asked her, "Mary, do you think you can make it ten squares?" Proud of herself, she said, "I think I can." Chris steadied her and helped her get started. Mary began to pedal with confidence and a smile on her face, and as she hit square after square on the sidewalk, not only did we cheer but also strangers and neighbors on the bike path cheered as if LSU had just scored a touchdown against Alabama. As she hit each square, we shouted them out—5! 6! 7! 8! My momma heart was bursting with joy and pride.

Suddenly, though, as she approached the tenth square where I was standing, I saw the fear overtake her. She returned to her old routine of looking backwards and sideways, and as she did, her bike began wobbling again, swooping side to side and swerving all over the place. Tears formed in her eyes. Seeing my child's fear, I ran up to her and got down low and caught her eyes. I said, "Mary, look at me. Look right here at me. Keep your eyes on me." Her eyes caught mine as I ran backwards to keep her moving. She steadied her eyes on me, and as she locked on the eyes of one who loves her dearly, something came over her that I will never forget as a mother. She steadied and stilled. And as she kept her eyes on the fixed point of one who loves her, her confidence grew. Her bike stopped swerving, and she sat straighter in the seat, and began pedaling with the confidence of a skilled bike rider. She hit the tenth square and everyone whooped and hollered and celebrated. The biggest grin broke out on her face and tears formed in my own eyes as I kept running to try to keep up with her as she hit square 11! 12! 13! 14! 15! At fifteen squares, I stopped running as she passed me up and kept going all the way back home.

I stood for a minute in complete silence with tears rolling down my face for the depth of love I have for my daughter, for understanding the power a mother's love has for a child, and for realizing the responsibility I have as her mother to be one of *her* still points. It overwhelmed me. How could I be her still point that steadied and stilled her without having my own still point? Not only did I need my own still point, but I also wanted to point my children to that still point.

What she taught me in that moment, in a profound way, is how we all need a still point in this world of busyness, tiredness, restlessness, wobbliness, fear, and so much more. Thankfully, we have a still point: Jesus.

Our pastor, Fr. Randy, has a painting in his office with the words, *Jesus is the still point in the turning world of chaos.* In the busy world we live in, we have a lived promise who is our still point: Jesus. Jesus, the long-promised Messiah to God's people, came. He lived in this world and offered people rest, refreshment, and recovery of strength. He was people's still point. He still is and can be your still point today.

Let's turn now to how we can be still and embrace the still point within us.

Be Still and Know

One of my favorite coffee mugs to use each morning is the one my friend Ann gave me when my first book was published. It is a beautiful white ceramic mug with a gold handle, and in beautiful gold letters are the words *Be still and know*. These four words are from Psalm 46:10: "Be still, and know that I am God." Often in the quiet of the mornings as I hold this mug in my hands, feel its warmth, and breathe deeply in the quiet, I am overwhelmed with gratitude that someone taught me that the inner chapel existed in the first place. As I still my body, embrace the silence, and go to my inner chapel, I lean in to the source of my rest and also the source of my daily strength. This daily stopping to be still and to know that God is there continues to transform my life.

When I pause each morning and go to my inner chapel, I access what Francis Vanderwall describes as the "fountain of living water" within us.

> This process is what is called prayer. It is an awakening to the realization that we are not alone, to the recognition that we are dearly loved and have a tender, caring, compassionate companion in Jesus our Lord. It is the attentive listening to the whispers of love that can be heard from the depths of our very own being, reassuring us of our own intrinsic worth. It is the understanding of what it means to have within ourselves the fountain of living water, ever bubbling up fresh and sparkling, to refresh us and renew us with its life giving properties.[10]

So many Scriptures give us clear direction on where our renewal comes from, Scriptures such as

- Psalm 23 // "Beside still waters he leads me and restores my soul."
- Psalm 62 // "In God alone is my soul at rest."
- Isaiah 58:9–11 // "The LORD will guide you continually, and satisfy your needs in parched places."

When we take moments to be still and go to our inner chapel and soak up the promises of God, we are refreshed, renewed, and

---

10. Francis W. Vanderwall, SJ, *Water in the Wilderness* (New York: Paulist Press, 1985), 3.

strengthened. We bring what God poured into us out into the world, our relationships, and our tasks. The living water within us nourishes us in all the places we are dry and in need of refreshment and strength.

God Recovers Our Strength

God helps us recover our strength, and God promises that our burden will be easy. This type of rest God promises was incredibly comforting to me as I walked with my grandfather. The worry and additional role in my life of walking with him combined with my normal responsibilities felt incredibly heavy at times.

The Scripture Matthew 11:28–30 brought me much comfort. I often remembered a homily I heard once in which the priest unpacked what this Scripture meant. During Jesus' time, when a young calf was yoked up for the first time, the older ox, because of its size, carried the bulk of the load, while the young calf's load was light. The two oxen (one older and wiser and the other younger and learning the way) were yoked together to walk the same path. The older ox carried the heavier load as the younger one was taught the way.

Jesus is always the older ox for us. Jesus yokes up to us and helps us carry what we are carrying. Because we are the young calf, Jesus gives us the lighter end. Jesus gives us respite and allows our strength to endure because our load is being lightened.

Even with knowing this promise is there for us, we still try to carry the burden on our own. Our culture applauds individualism, independence, and "self-help" mentality. While there are elements of these philosophies that are good, they propose that we are left to this world by ourselves. It seems we celebrate those who push ahead and survive due to their own personal gumption, strength, or perseverance. How often do we take pride in doing something ourselves or accomplishing it on our own? I can think of dozens of examples where this thinking guided my journey. Moments like trying to solve a complex problem by myself, learning to love myself, or forgiving someone on my own. My energy and perseverance lasted for a short time, but after a while of carrying it on my own, I got weary and found myself sputtering like an engine completely out of gas.

Sometimes, we resist allowing God to be part of our process because it means giving up control and surrendering. It makes us feel good and safe when we feel we are in control or when we have all the pieces and parts in our hands. It can make us feel good about ourselves that we can do something on our own. In so many ways, when we don't allow God to help carry our burden, pride rules the day. Pride to me is ultimately saying, "I trust myself more than you, God." Let me tell you from experience that it's much easier to let God into situations, to stand shoulder to shoulder with Jesus, and to not go it alone. Letting go is not an easy thing to do, but when we do, we give God room to come in the most unexpected ways and offer rest, strength, and nourishment.

God Carries Us in Prayer

Sometimes we are so tired we can hardly show up in prayer. We may have a desire to be there but not the energy to offer prayers. That is when we can lean on the promise of the Advocate, the Holy Spirit, who will aid us in our weakness and who groans on our behalf: "Likewise the Spirit helps us in our weakness; for we do not know how to pray as we ought, but that very Spirit intercedes with sighs too deep for words"(Romans 8:26).

I can think of times when weariness overcame me, and I felt I could no longer pray. In those moments, I asked the Holy Spirit to pray for me. God, through the Holy Spirit, gives us what we need. Prayer is like water coming into a dry sponge that is stiff. As the living waters of God enter our hearts, they soften and moisten us, replenishing those thirsty, arid places, softening us to receive what God seeks to offer us.

Rest comes to us in prayer in all kinds of ways. God who sees us gives us what we need even when we do not know we need it. God pours into us the theological virtues of faith, hope, and love. These three have their source in God alone. We cannot have faith without God. We do not love without God. We do not hope without God. All it takes is for us to show up in the inner chapel with honesty and share with God what we long for. God opens us to receive the theological virtues, also fruits of the Holy Spirit.

The following examples come from others' stories, as I have listened to them and watched God carry them in prayer.

A woman I met with on a retreat was feeling very concerned about the weight of financial decisions. Carrying it by herself made her feel very tired. As she went to her inner chapel one morning, God reminded her simply that "I am God and I am with you." This understanding that she was not alone relieved her and enabled her to carry on with a trust that God saw her and would help her.

A man tired and anxious about choices in his past began going to his inner chapel daily, and God offered him a drink from the fountain of living water by comforting him through words of Scripture that reminded him that he was worthy of God's love just as he was and that mercy was available for him. As he drank these promises, his faith was restored, and he felt peace and hope.

A woman noticed she had less energy teaching after many years in the classroom. She brought the question of what were her next steps to her inner chapel, and God renewed her energy to finish the year and gave her clarity about her next steps.

God is the source of our rest. Our part is to *be still*, to *know* God is there, and to *drink* from the fountain of living water within us. We receive this gift of rest from the inner chapel. Rest comes by pausing and being still and learning that in the silence and stillness we come to know God.

If I am honest, I do not know what I would do or what my life would look like without visiting my inner chapel every morning. Each day begins with a visit to my inner chapel, and from this daily pausing to be with God, I drink from the fountain of living water and draw the strength I need for my day ahead.

As *Evangelii Gaudium* says,

> What is needed is the ability to cultivate an interior space which can give a Christian meaning to commitment and activity. Without prolonged moments of adoration, of prayerful encounter with the word, of sincere conversation with the Lord, our work easily becomes meaningless; we lose energy as a result of weariness and difficulties, and our fervor dies out.[11]

Resting in God daily by pausing and being still with God continually renews our energy and allows us to recover our strength for our day-to-day responsibilities.

Sabbath Taking Today: Rituals of Rest

On one hand I know I have a role in carving out time for rest, and on the other, I savor the promise of Jesus' words, "*I will give you rest.*" I know that rest is not mine to do alone, but I also understand that to receive rest I have to slow down and take sabbath moments.

In Hebrews, we find words of this promise of rest for God's people.

> So then, a sabbath rest still remains for the people of God; for those who enter God's rest also cease from their labors as God did from his. (Hebrews 4:9–10)

---

11. Pope Francis, *The Joy of the Gospel (Evangelii Gaudium)* (USCCB: Washington, D.C., 2013), #262.

This special rest is available to each one of us. It's a promise that God and Jesus model, and it is offered to us as well. God rested on the seventh day of creation.

> And on the seventh day God finished the work that he had done, and he rested on the seventh day from all the work that he had done. So God blessed the seventh day and hallowed it, because on it God rested from all the work that he had done in creation. (Genesis 2:2–3)

In the Gospel of Mark, we see an example of Jesus talking about the need for rest.

> The apostles gathered around Jesus, and told him all that they had done and taught. He said to them, "Come away to a deserted place all by yourselves and rest a while." For many were coming and going, and they had no leisure even to eat. And they went away in the boat to a deserted place by themselves. (6:30–32)

Several years ago, I spoke at a conference for spiritual directors. One day I sat with a group of my friends and fellow spiritual directors at lunch. The conversation at the table turned to how to take a sabbath in our lives. At the time, my oldest two children were five and three. Many around the table did not have children and spoke of taking off an entire day a week for a sabbath day.

To be honest, I was envious of their ability to take off a whole day every week, and I could feel my resentment grow as I listened to the conversation. My interior monologue was going ninety to nothing as I thought of the basic tasks that would never go away for me as a parent if I tried to take a sabbath day: laundry, meals, baths, homework time, carpooling kids, and the basic care of children. Even on weekends and evenings when work "ended," there was a mile-long list of tasks that needed to be done to care for the beautiful little human beings in our home.

I could feel the disconnect between what I was hearing and my life as a parent. I recognized my growing resentment, and I wanted to scream, "You just don't get it!" The frustration and anger were familiar; I'd experienced them often, especially in my life as a minister. Often the way sabbath and prayer are talked about, even by some of the authors and ministers I read diligently and respect and listen to the most, they are presented as far-off goals a person can achieve later in life or if he or she has no children.

I knew already that there *was* a way to be still daily and to make time for prayer, my foundational rest, because by this point I'd used a daily practice for almost fifteen years. Even with my frustration, I could feel God affirming my call yet again to help people know that they *can* make space for prayer even with work, with marriages, and with children. That day, though, I could not for the life of me figure out how to make time for longer rest and a sabbath in my life.

A friend, sensing my frustration, asked me what was going on. I shared how I felt that the longer rest and taking sabbath they were talking about could not fit into my life. That to check out for a whole day once a week was not possible due to caring for children. She then asked me, "What if you thought about sabbath in another way?" Could I think of rest as "Renewing Energy in Spirit Time"?

As she shared more about what it meant to her to rest and renew energy in spirit time, she encouraged me to think about moments in my day and week when I could incorporate rituals of rest instead of taking an entire day for a sabbath. She encouraged me to look for moments that allowed God to renew my spirit, and she reminded me of Jesus' words in Matthew's Gospel, "Come to me, all you that are weary and are carrying heavy burdens, and I will give you rest" (11:28).

Lunch ended, and I continued to chew on this new idea of rest.

In our world that is so busy and fast-paced, this first aspect of rest—ceasing movement—could not be more important. It is hard to receive the promised and available gift of rest if we do not cease our movement. This means stilling not only our bodies but also our minds. To lean in to this promised rest, we can create boundaries to help us cease movement, such as putting down our phones, setting time limits for technology, limiting the amount of work we bring home with us because of the e-mails and texts coming constantly into our hands and minds.

As a parent, I often think of the differences between parenting now and when my parents raised me. While there are many changes, one of the biggest things I notice is that when my parents physically left work, they were able to come home without lugging e-mails and texts about work with them. The afternoon and evening times for a parent were not much different then, but people were not attempting to focus on family life at the same time they were addressing the texts and e-mails from work coming in at all hours of the night. I have caught myself trying to deal with e-mail and voicemail while shuttling my kids from place to place, texting answers in one parking lot before heading to another one. The pressure of work is steady and constant.

I shared the idea of renewing energy in spirit time with Chris. The two of us began to look at our lives and discern ways to incorporate rituals of rest that renewed energy in spirit time into our days, weeks, and months. Many of these rituals we still incorporate today. They helped us seek rest in the middle of life with kids, work, and journeying with my grandfather.

Here are examples of a few of our rituals that renew our energy in spirit time. You will see that some are specifically spiritual, but there are also some that simply invite us to engage in rest through the spirit of play and togetherness.

- **Daily prayer.** I have shared at length about this, but this daily foundational rest is something Chris and I value tremendously. We give each other time for daily prayer and we also make time for moments of prayer as a family.

- **Pancake Saturday or Sunday.** We try our best to give ourselves one slow morning each weekend where everyone stays in their pajamas longer and someone cooks pancakes. While it used to be my husband who was the pancake chef, this is now something my older two children love to do on these mornings.

- **Attending Mass every Sunday.** We make the commitment as a family each Sunday to pause and be together with our community of faith. Slowing down to pray with others, to celebrate and remember what Jesus did for us, and to be renewed by the Eucharist each week is a vital aspect of rest in our lives.

- **Family movie night.** At least once or twice a month, we do not schedule any activities on a weekend night, and everyone piles onto the couch in pajamas to watch a movie and eat pizza.

- **Reading.** Our family loves to read. Often, we just give ourselves permission to curl up in the chair of our choice and slip away into whatever book we are enjoying.

- **Spending time in nature.** We all enjoy being outdoors. So we make time to be in the sun, whether that is through playing outside, biking, walking our dog, or gardening.

- **Play and hobbies.** There is nothing better than giving yourself permission to just play or pursue something you enjoy. We try to encourage this spirit of play both as a family and also individually, based on what people like to do.

- **Listening to music.** We like to have spontaneous dance parties in our kitchen or while working on other tasks. The music lifts our spirits.

- **Attending an annual retreat.** Chris and I support each other's desire for intentional time with God each year on a silent retreat. This longer time of rest renews each of us.

What might be some of your rituals of rest?

Cut the Ballast

I want to share one last thought that I think is important to understand about the promise of rest for the weary. We need to give ourselves permission to put down things that are no longer ours to do.

The last month my grandfather was in hospice was a hard time. His health was declining quickly, and I wanted to spend every minute I could with him. He also needed extra care and attention. That month, I had several local retreats and also national ones on the calendar, all scheduled long before we knew where my grandfather would be in his health journey. I had planned to host a friend's baby shower that month. Life had all its normal responsibilities also.

The grief of what we were about to face with the loss of my grandfather weighed heavy on me, and I began to notice that daily tasks were becoming more difficult to complete. I also noticed I was having trouble sleeping. Often I could not fall asleep, and when I did sleep, I slept fitfully and often woke up in the middle of the night. I noticed, too, that I was feeling very anxious, no doubt because of the anticipated death of my dear grandfather; all signs were pointing to it being sooner rather than later.

Noticing signs that had shown up during other times of exhaustion and near burnout, I called a friend and neighbor who was a counselor and who had accompanied his father through terminal cancer years before. I shared with him what was going on, and his advice to me was, "Cut the ballast."

On a ship, ballast is material that keeps the vessel in balance and allows the weight to be distributed so it can move forward without sinking. Sometimes more weight is added so the ship won't tip over, and sometimes weight is taken away so the ship doesn't sink. They call that cutting ballast. My friend invited me to take a hard look at what my commitments were and to cut anything that was not needed so that I could focus on my greater priorities of caring for my grandfather, spending the last days with him, and continuing the normal family tasks that could not stop. In terms of work, what was coming up on the calendar? What retreats or events could wait until another time? Which events should be canceled because I simply did not have the mental capacity to do them well right now?

Using his wisdom, I canceled all my retreats scheduled that month. Every person I called to tell what was going on understood and was very supportive. I stopped writing my blog for that month. I also called my friend and let her know that I simply could not host her baby shower at that time. She graciously understood and walked with me the entire time of my grandfather's illness.

Chris and I took a hard look at our kids' schedules and commitments and also cut out anything that did not support the greater priorities at that time.

I'm not going to lie: This was not an easy thing to do, as I pride myself on being someone people can rely on. When I give my word, I mean it and keep it. All kinds of mom guilt crept in as we backed out of sports teams and other activities my kids were already signed up for. We cut everything we could and left the bare minimum.

Freeing myself and our family of all the extras gave us more time and space and permission to spend extra time with my grandfather. I will never regret this decision. I would not trade one minute of the time I got to spend with him and the time Chris and our children spent with him. We had heartfelt conversations—during that time, Boppy shared with me the words that open this book.

I also would have missed how deeply God was tending to my grandfather in his inner chapel in those last few weeks and readying him to meet God.

Cutting the ballast to make time for the greatest priorities of our life is wisdom we can all apply when we notice our tiredness. While we might not need to cut back to the extreme the way Chris and I did at that particular time, we can simply cut the extra things that are keeping us from our greatest priorities. Where might God be offering you rest by helping you know it is time to cut the ballast?

What about You?

What part of this promise of God do you need to cling to right now? Are you being invited to include sabbath moments in your week? Are you being invited to linger beside still waters to be refreshed? Is God reminding you that you are not alone as you carry your load? Or are you being called to be the hands and arms of God by offering others rest right now? Whatever you feel called to, I invite you to put it into action and lean in to the promise of God's rest.

LET'S GO TO THE INNER CHAPEL

Parched Land Meditation

> The LORD will guide you continually, / and satisfy your needs in parched places, / and make your bones strong; / and you shall be like a watered garden, / like a spring of water, / whose waters never fail. (Isaiah 58:11)

Close your eyes and go to your inner chapel. Imagine that you and Jesus are surveying your life together, noticing the places in your life that are "sun-scorched"—dry and arid. Together, you notice all the places that are in need of water. Imagine you and Jesus walking up to each parched area of your life. Talk to Jesus about what you see. Listen to what he tells you about this area of your life. Then, watch as Jesus pours his living water into this sun-scorched area of your life. What does the living water look like that he pours? How does his gift of water satisfy your thirst? How does it renew and restore the dry land?

Creating Rituals of Rest

I invite you to create your own rituals of rest that "renew energy in spirit time."

- **Foundational rest.** What will your daily prayer time look like? What will be your time of prayer? Place of prayer? How can you make it a sacred space?

- **Daily rituals of rest.** What are daily rituals of rest that honor our need to cease movement, refresh, and recover strength?

- **Weekly rituals of rest.** What weekly rhythms do you want to incorporate into your life to lean in to God's promise of rest for the weary?

- **Monthly rituals of rest.** Are there any monthly rituals you want to consider making part of your life?

- **Yearly rituals of rest.** Are there yearly rituals of rest such as a retreat or a set time away that you would like to begin including as part of your year?

Embracing the Promises of God

These Scriptures can encourage you as you read them and pray with them.

- Psalm 63:1–9 // "My soul thirsts for you; / my flesh faints for you, / as in a dry and weary land where there is no water."
- Ezekiel 37:1–14 // The valley of dry bones
- Jeremiah 17:7–8 // "Blessed are those who trust in the LORD, / whose trust is the LORD. / They shall be like a tree planted by water."

9

We Can Find Shelter
and Intimacy

We long to be loved, to be known, to be seen, and to belong. We yearn for security and something solid that transcends the multitude of transitions and changes that we face. For as long as I can remember, my grandmother shared with me the wisdom that "one of the things you can count on in life is change." How true this statement is! We face continual changes. We elect new officials every year in the various levels of government. Our friendships change as life's seasons cycle through stages. Jobs change. Seasons change. People are born and people die. Our moods change: we laugh, we cry, we get angry, we get sad, we get lonely. Where we live changes as we move and relocate. Our families change, expanding by adding children or shrinking because of the loss of a loved one. Even the closest relationships can experience brief moments or long spans of brokenness and hurt.

Grandmother's spoken words of wisdom about change are absolutely true. Her wisdom about change, however, does not stop there. So often, not through spoken word but by her example, she is an authentic witness to what holds us steady through the inevitable changes we face: a relationship with God. She modeled this as she walked alongside my grandfather, never giving up hope, by turning again and again to the source of her strength. Her steadfastness in faith as she watched her spouse suffer and embraced change after change in her life reminded me of where to find strength for the changes that will surely come on my own journey.

About ten days before my grandfather died, I spent the rare night at their home to keep vigil with my grandmother and the night sitter because of the breathing changes my grandfather had experienced earlier in the day. I normally was at their home only during the day to allow them sacred time together as a couple and also to allow me time to be with my husband and children. Being there that night allowed me to witness a profound act of love and intimacy. As we began settling in for the night, I watched my grandmother's routine unfold. The sitter put her chair at the foot of my grandfather's bed. Then she grabbed the ottoman for my grandmother to rest her feet on. My grandmother grabbed the blanket she used each night that had a pocket for her to tuck her feet into to keep warm. Lights were strategically turned off or left on to allow for tending to my grandfather in the middle of the night while providing my grandmother dim enough light to sleep.

My spot for the vigil that night was a maroon recliner positioned behind my grandmother's chair. As I settled in, I was in a unique position to observe the beauty of a sixty-five-year-old marriage. They kissed good night. One lying in bed fighting for his life. One (despite my efforts to get her to move into a bed for the evening) lovingly sitting upright in her chair to be near him, sacrificing the comfort of a bed to do so. I knew I was witnessing an example of God's love as I watched them. The intimacy they shared that night reflected glimpses of God's intimacy with us. This intimacy was life-long, sustaining, hopeful, tender, and it held a trust in each other that encompassed both joy and sorrow. Their love, though, found its source in what they both did next.

As they settled into their places of physical rest that night, they carried out a practice I had watched them do hundreds of times, from my days as a child sleeping over at their house. This practice was one we participated in together and did verbally. This night, though, no words were spoken or exchanged among us. They both made the sign of the cross, leaned back, closed their eyes, and quietly went into their inner chapels. I felt God's presence so clearly in this moment that held authentic love and expectant sorrow that my eyes filled with tears and rolled down my cheeks. I made my own sign of the cross, leaned back in my chair, closed my eyes, and quietly went to my inner chapel too. While I could not hear their prayers that night, I prayed for them and with them. I did not know what the night would hold, based on the day's changes, but I embraced the gift of knowing that none of us was alone no matter what as we took shelter in God.

Change Is Not Life's Only Constant

Even though life changes, there *is* a constant other than change. Throughout the centuries, there is a steady, unshakable, consistent, enduring presence in our world: God. Through the ages and all human development, God remains. Throughout our salvation story, we can see God's consistency and steadiness in human experience. Humans have changed in their understanding of God, but God has always remained. We need only look to Scripture to see God's revelation to humans in different ways. God invites Abram to look at the sky and count the stars, and by doing so, reveals a plan to Abram that his descendants will be as numerous as the stars (Genesis 15). Moses comes to understand God's presence through the burning bush (Exodus 3), and later his understanding about God grows while on Mount Sinai. There God revealed the Ten Commandments, which were to serve as a sign of God's covenant with God's People (Exodus 20). Later, we witness God's revelation to Jeremiah: God will move the law from words on stone to wisdom written on the human heart (Jeremiah 31:33). God's presence endures in the world through all these moments in our salvation history.

One of my favorite psalms is 136. It is a psalm in praise of God's enduring love through the centuries. The line "His steadfast love endures forever" is repeated many times, reminding us that no matter what, God's presence and gift of love endure. Throughout the centuries, God spoke to people from their inner chapels. God's presence in their lives helped them endure many things. What I witnessed that night with my grandparents as I kept vigil reminded me that God's love was enduring still.

Scripture shows us God's desire for relationship with us. Never wanting only a superficial relationship, God sought *intimacy* with us. God seeks intimacy with us now. We are not different from the people in the Scriptures. We are women at the well harboring secrets that God already knows and we yearn to share. We are blind men yearning for sight. We are the lost son hoping that our absence will be noticed. We are Naomi and Ruth clinging to each other after mourning multiple deaths. We are Sarah without a child. In each of these situations, God encounters people and offers them the gift of relationship and spiritual intimacy. God offers this gift to us, too.

Shelter in God

We live at a time in which many of the institutions we once trusted have broken that trust. At the same time that trusted institutions seem to be falling apart, it appears that the world is becoming more chaotic and broken as we watch violence of all kinds increase. I often feel stuck between the desire to stay informed by watching the news and the desire to be an ostrich sticking my head in the sand and avoiding the news. The news does not feel like a safe show to have on in my home because of the overflow of negative news that can arouse fear in my children. Not to mention the utter feeling of hopelessness it can cause in me as I watch system after system fail individuals and communities. At times, I despair for my children's futures.

How many mothers who went before me, though, felt these same feelings welling up as they heard news of violence in their neighborhoods or around the world? How many mothers around this globe today are facing situations far graver than what I am staring at in my own South Louisiana world? Mothers who are fighting not only for their children's lives but also for their own lives and rights? It is during times like these that the work of the evil one is most at play, making us feel stuck, hopeless, and alone. Maybe you feel this way as you read these words and think about the many concerns in your private life and in the larger world.

But did you know that we are not the only ones seeing the world and all that is happening? We are not the only eyes witnessing world events and feeling deep sorrow for the loss of life, the brokenness of our world, and the chaos caused by human choices. We are not alone. God sees the world. God sees us. God sees you.

God sees us the same way God saw the struggles, plights, and hardships of people throughout all of salvation history. God saw Elijah as he fled for his life and as he sat beneath the broom tree in exasperation and cried out, "Enough, Lord!" The Lord saw him there and saw his exhaustion and fear and sent a messenger who awoke him and said, "Get up and eat!" Elijah was strengthened by that food to walk another forty days and nights to the mountain of God (1 Kings 19:1–8). God saw Elijah and sheltered him by giving him what he needed to continue on.

God sees us the same way God saw the plight of Hagar, maid of Sarai, who had conceived a son with Abraham and was so mistreated by Sarai that she ran away. Hagar felt she was abandoned by the family she belonged to and was in despair. As Scripture says, the Lord's angel found her in the wilderness and asked her, "Hagar, slave-girl of Sarai, where have you come from and where are you going?" God saw her, comforted her, and offered her a promise of shelter and relief from her suffering. Hagar spoke to the Lord and gave a name to God: "You are El-roi," meaning *you are God who sees me* (Genesis 16:13).

God saw Elijah and Hagar. God sees each one of us. In the Scriptures are many more examples of God seeing people and their need in times of distress, abandonment, exhaustion, and hopelessness and offering them the shelter they need at that moment. This promise of God did not stop when the Bible concluded. This promise is as relevant to us today as it was thousands of years ago. God is to each of us the One who sees.

We don't always understand in the moment that God sees us or shelters us. Sometimes it requires pausing and looking back on our life and asking ourselves the questions God posed to Hagar.

- Where have you come from?
- Where are you going?

It helps to pause and look back on our life and notice where we have come from and how God was part of it in ways we did not initially understand while we were living it. Reflecting on this helps increase our faith and trust in God and helps us understand where we are *now* going. As Hagar understood that God saw her and comforted her, she was able to better understand where she was going and returned home and bore Abram a son.

As a wise woman named Katie shared with me on a retreat I was facilitating, "Thus far, we have survived 100 percent of our worst days." If you are reading this book, you have survived 100 percent of your worst days.

I invite you to look back over your life now. Where are you coming from? Where are you going? Are there moments it might be helpful to reflect on and notice how God sheltered you in unexpected ways? How might this promise of God's shelter have been part of your life?

Let's turn now to a meditation St. Ignatius offers that helps us understand that God sees us.

St. Ignatius's Meditation on the Incarnation

St. Ignatius offers us a meditation that reminds us that God sees the world, sees us, and sees what is happening. In this meditation he invites us to reflect on the Trinity: Father, Son, and Holy Spirit, looking down on the world and noticing. Here are his words:

> Looking upon our world: men and women being born and being laid to rest, some getting married and others getting divorced, the old and the young, the rich and the poor, the happy and the sad, so many people aimless, despairing, hateful, and killing, so many undernourished, sick, and dying, so many struggling with life and blind to any meaning. With God, I can hear people laughing and crying, some shouting and screaming, some praying, others cursing.[12]

Every time I read these words and guide people through this part of the *Spiritual Exercises*, I think, *This sounds all too familiar.* St. Ignatius penned these words over five hundred years ago, but they ring true today. Are people not being born and dying? Are people not getting married and divorced? Are there not young and old, rich and poor, the happy and the sad? Are people not aimless? Despairing? Hateful and killing? Are we not faced with an overwhelming part of our world's

---

12. David L. Fleming, SJ, *Draw Me into Your Friendship: A Literal Translation and a Contemporary Reading of the Spiritual Exercises* (St. Louis: Institute of Jesuit Sources, 1996), 91.

population who are undernourished, sick, dying, and struggling with life? Are people not laughing, crying, shouting, screaming, some praying while others are cursing?

What St. Ignatius noticed five hundred years ago is not much different from today. What he imagined the Trinity seeing back then is not much different from what the Trinity sees today. St. Ignatius saw the world groaning, just as we are groaning now. His reflection continues.

> In a leap of divine joy: God knows that the time has come when the mystery of salvation, hidden from the beginning of the world, will shine into human darkness and confusion. It is as if I can hear the Divine Persons saying, "Let us work the redemption of the whole human race; let us respond to the groaning of all creation."[13]

The ultimate response to the groaning of creation is the decision to send an angel to Mary (Luke 1:26–38). Mary's yes puts into motion the Incarnation, God becoming flesh and "[living] among us" (John 1:14). Mary sheltered God within her in the form of Jesus. At the same time that Mary was sheltering Jesus, she was also sheltered by God who saw her and was with her in her inner chapel. They were inseparable from each other. God sought to shelter us by sheltering *with* us.

We see intimacy here: God's response to the groaning of the world began with the tenderness of a mother who first said yes and then received her child in her arms. Can you imagine the gaze between mother and child that day? Mary gazing into Jesus' tiny eyes, stroking his hair, and snuggling the new life in her arms. Mary feeling the same profound love, tremendous responsibility, and fear that all new parents experience. Jesus looking up at her. Jesus crying and

---

13. Fleming, *Draw Me into Your Friendship*, 91–92.

needing to be soothed by his mother, the same way all newborns need to be soothed.

Having received three babies in my arms, my guess is that Mary was changed the day Jesus was born. I physically sheltered my children in me as Mary did Jesus. The moment my son, Brady, was first placed into my arms, everything changed. As I gazed into his eyes, stroked his peach-fuzz hair, and snuggled new life, I knew my life would never be the same. I knew my life would be consumed with loving him, protecting him, sheltering him. I knew, as I held him, that I would experience love in a way I had never experienced it before. When Abby was placed in my arms two years later, my life changed again because my heart expanded with love for her, and the same deep-down desire to protect and shelter her arose. When Mary was placed in my arms five years later, I understood that love could expand beyond what I could imagine. That same desire welled up within to love, to shelter, and to protect her. Parents across the world understand the emotional moment of receiving our children into our arms for the first time. In an instant, there is a fleeting range of emotions that go from profound love for another to fear at the tremendous responsibility given to shelter and protect one you love so fiercely.

There is an intimacy I can understand as a mother of three children. There is a deep connection to my children. They are known to me. Their ways are familiar to me. What I feel for them, while stunningly beautiful, does not come close to how known we are to God and how familiar God is with each one of us. It is only through returning time and time again to my inner chapel to be with God that I come to understand even in the smallest of ways what it means to live in spiritual intimacy with God.

Can you imagine what spiritual intimacy looked like for Mary and God? I wonder how many times she embraced the gift of her inner chapel as she pondered what she noticed about her Son. I believe in my gut that Mary must have understood the gift of intimacy that comes with friendship with God that St. Teresa of Ávila captures:

> Here's what a friendship with our dearest Companion, our holiest God, is like. In it, intimacy is always possible and cannot be stopped, except on our side, for God is always open to us. Nothing can come between us and God, our Spouse, and we can be alone with God whenever we want, as long as we want. All we have to do is desire it.
>
> So let us close the door on our worldly calendars and deadlines and live instead in paradise with the God of love. If we desire this closeness that comes from closing the door on the world, we must realize that the door is our hearts. We don't have to be mystics to accomplish this communion. We only need to focus on God with our will. That's all. It's our own choice, and because God loves us, we can do this. Don't confuse this state with empty silence. I am speaking of a turning inward and a listening.[14]

I invite you to learn what St. Teresa of Ávila speaks of here and what I have come to discover through the years of going to the inner chapel every day: the gift of shelter and intimacy.

Spiritual Intimacy

I often hear people share in spiritual direction and on retreats how much they desire intimacy with someone. Intimacy is defined by Webster's dictionary as "a close, familiar, and usually affectionate or loving personal relationship with another person or group" or "a close association with or detailed knowledge or deep understanding of a place, subject, period of history, etc." or "the quality of being comfortable, warm, or familiar." I believe that we all want to be loved, to

---

14. Carmen Acevedo Butcher, *A Little Daily Wisdom: Christian Women Mystics* (Brewster, MA: Paraclete Press, 2008), 69.

be familiar to someone, and to have our stories and lives known in a deep way by another person. The most utter despair and hopelessness that I witness in people is when they are going through life without an intimate relationship with another person. This loneliness, disconnection, and isolation at times can pull us to a dark place.

As our culture changes and technology evolves, we are becoming a society with less intimacy with other people, less connection, less community, and steady change. Due to the continuous change, we have fewer moments of stabilization in our society, which means that it's rare to get a moment to pause, catch our breath, reset, and check in on who we actually are.

What if I told you that there was one thing that didn't change? What if I told you there was one relationship in your life that was steady and consistent and offered you a place of intimacy that far surpasses anything another person can offer? Would it possibly impact the way you walk through life? Would your hope increase a bit, knowing that whatever you are facing or dealing with, you are not meeting it alone?

God invites us to embrace the gift of spiritual intimacy. Monty Williams, SJ, in his book *The Gift of Spiritual Intimacy*, defines spiritual intimacy as our "truest sense of our selves [as] inseparably rooted in God."[15] Let that sink in a moment. The deepest intimacy we long for is not defined through being in relationship with another person, not through what we own or what we do. This depth of being known, seen, loved, worthy, secure, and familiar to someone finds its roots in God's tenacious love for us.

Williams goes on to say, "The gift of such radical intimacy is offered to all. It is a gift we are free to accept or to refuse. Should we

---

15. Monty Williams, SJ, *The Gift of Spiritual Intimacy: Following the Spiritual Exercises of Saint Ignatius* (Toronto: Novalis, 2009), 11.

accept, we are further invited to open, use, share, and finally celebrate that gift." Put another way, God's offer of divine love and intimate relationship with us is never withdrawn. Even if we are unaware of it, God is still there.

This is the promise of God that Psalm 136 so passionately proclaims repeatedly: "His steadfast love endures forever." God offers us the invitation to open ourselves to God's love, to embrace the gift of God's love, and to accept that we cannot be separated from God. This is truly the gift of God's mercy, which we will unpack in depth later in this book. God will never stop initiating and attempting to draw us into a relationship. God will continue to woo and pursue us.

Inseparable from God

I want to turn to a more modern example of what it means to be inseparably rooted in God. I recently read the profound and moving autobiography of Immaculée Ilibagiza called *Left to Tell: Discovering God amidst the Rwandan Holocaust*. Immaculée is a survivor of the Rwandan Genocide that occurred in 1994. While she survived, her family and other members of the Tutsi tribe were massacred by another tribe, the Hutu.

Immaculée shares that she lived in a locked bathroom for three months with six other women, hiding there to escape the mass killings. The space was tight and cramped. The seven women could hardly move around. As she hid in the dark bathroom, she knew that many of her family members had already been killed and that she was being hunted. Her home was burned to the ground. She had lost everything except her faith:

> I found a place in the bathroom to call my own: a small corner of my heart. I retreated there as soon as I awoke and stayed there until I slept. It was my sacred garden, where I spoke with God, meditated on His words, and nurtured my spiritual self. When

I meditated, I touched the source of my faith and strengthened the core of my soul. While horror swirled around me, I found refuge in a world that became more welcoming and wonderful each visit. Even as my body shriveled, my soul was nourished through my deepening relationship with God. I entered my space through prayer; once inside, I prayed nonstop.[16]

Immaculée found shelter and refuge in God. God saw her in her suffering, abandonment, and despair. At one point of utter despair, she found refuge in the words of Psalm 91.

> This I declare, that He alone is my refuge, my place of safety; He is my God, and I am trusting Him. For He rescues you from every trap and protects you from the fatal plague. He will shield you with His wings! They will shelter you. His faith promises are your armor. Now you don't need to be afraid of the dark anymore, nor fear the dangers of the day; nor dread the plagues of darkness, nor disasters in the morning.
>
> Though a thousand fall at my side, though ten thousand are dying around me, the evil will not touch me.[17]

She never lost her faith as she surrendered and retreated into her shelter within, her inner chapel. She knew that by going there, she was never abandoned or alone. She leaned on these promises of shelter and intimacy with God. She embraced the promise of being inseparable from God, and this allowed her to endure tragedy, loss, and utter despair. Even when all else was stripped from her, she embraced her foundational identity that was secure in knowing she was a woman loved by God.

---

16. Immaculée Ilibagiza, *Left to Tell: Discovering God amidst the Rwandan Holocaust* (Carlsbad, CA: Hay House, 2006), chapter 12 in e-book.
17. Ilibagiza, *Left to Tell*, chapter 12 in e-book.

Identity in God

Most of us will not face the extreme circumstances that Immaculée did. How often, though, do we search for what defines us? Humans are on a relentless pursuit to answer the question, "Who am I?" We define our identity in a multitude of ways: through what we do, what we own, who we are in relationship with, and where we live. I could easily boil my identity down to this: I am a South Louisiana native woman, a wife, a mother, a friend, a granddaughter, a daughter, a sister, a spiritual director, an author, and a retreat facilitator. I could even throw in things like, I am a huge LSU fan, an avid coffee drinker, a book collector. An endless list defines me.

What happens, though, if any of these things changes? What if I move out of Louisiana (happened to me for seven years)? Who am I then? What if there is a time when the work I am passionate about goes away and the roles of spiritual director, author, and retreat facilitator are paused—who am I then? This happens to many in times of great transition such as moving from one part of the country to another, giving birth to or adopting a baby, or starting a new job. Sometimes even strong relationships that define us change, and our once-secure selves change.

In our spiritual intimacy with God, we grow to understand that our identity is inseparable from our relationship with God. Our key, defining relationships with other people will change eventually, but our relationship with God is the core of who we are.

For instance, look at what happened at Jesus' baptism by John. Jesus, the Son of God, sees his cousin John the Baptist baptizing people in the river Jordan. Upon seeing this, Jesus approaches John to be baptized. Clearly aware that Jesus is the Messiah, John's response is, "I need to be baptized by you, and do you come to me?" (Matthew 3:14). In Luke's account of Jesus' baptism, it says

Now when all the people were baptized, and when Jesus also had been baptized and was praying, the heaven was opened, and the Holy Spirit descended upon him in bodily form like a dove. And a voice came from heaven, "You are my Son the Beloved; with you I am well pleased." (Luke 3:21–22)

In this profound moment of Jesus' baptism, God makes Jesus' identity clear. It is found in God's love. I wonder how this assurance in God's love changed Jesus. I wonder if Jesus, in his humanity, longed for a sense of who he was. God made it clear that Jesus' identity was inseparable from God's love. How might the gift of God's offer of love to Jesus have carried him through the rest of his life?

I can think of a time in my life when so many things that defined me changed. We had moved from my hometown of Baton Rouge, where I had lived for twenty-eight years. My son was sixteen months old, so the role of motherhood was still new to me. With the move, the ministry work I did in Baton Rouge ended, and I found myself in a city where there was not an immediate use of my gifts or passions for ministry work. I was far away from my family and life-long friends. The move's catalyst was Chris moving out of full-time work into a full-time graduate program. There was a moment in prayer that first year of our move when I cried out to God, "Who am I?" Everything had changed, and I did not know who I was. In the quiet of my inner chapel in the wee hours of the morning in a new home and new city, I heard similar words that Jesus heard at his baptism: "You are my beloved daughter. In you I am well pleased." In that moment, God spoke to me and awakened me to the truest sense of my identity. I was a beloved child of God. Those moments of prayer birthed a phrase that I repeated and prayed and clung to as I leaned further into life in a new city: *Who I am in God is who I am.*

For the past ten years, these nine words have grounded and calmed me when life threw its expected and unexpected changes my way. I still repeat this phrase often when I am feeling unsure of who I am. This was and is such a pivotal revelation to me by God that I had a friend paint *Who I am in God is who I am* on a small canvas; I hung it right next to my desk. As I type these words, I pause to remember the moment in prayer when God reminded me who I am, and I also remember the power these words held for me in many moments during the past decade, when it was easy to forget who I was. This phrase brings me home time and time again to remember that the truest sense of who I am is a woman inseparable from God.

This is the gift of spiritual intimacy with God. Our identity doesn't come from what we do, what role we play, where we live, or what we own, but simply from the person we are in God. This is true for each of us. This offer of the source of our identity is not found through our tasks, our goals, our ambitions, our relationships, or anything else, but in the fact that we are inseparable from God and therefore never alone.

LET'S GO TO THE INNER CHAPEL

How about you? Are you ready to go to your inner chapel? Are you ready to turn inward and listen to God's voice of love offering you companionship and friendship that shelter you and give you a sense of who you are?

Incarnation Meditation

Imagine the Trinity looking upon you and your life right now. What would they see? Where are you groaning and longing for someone to see what you are going through? Where are you hoping for shelter? In what aspects of your life would it help to embrace the promise of God's shelter and intimacy?

Hagar Meditation

Reflect on the questions God posed to Hagar. *Where are you coming from? Where are you going?*

Go to your inner chapel. As you settle into this special place of strength, shelter, and refuge, invite God to help you recall a time when you struggled to believe God saw you or was with you as you experienced it. As you reflect on it, ask God to show you ways that God saw you, sheltered you, and offered you what you needed to face the next thing.

Embracing the Promises of God

In addition to the ones listed throughout the chapter, here are a few more verses to help you lean on the promises of shelter and intimacy.

These Scriptures can encourage you as you read them and pray with them.

- Sirach 34:16–20 // "The eyes of the Lord are on those who love him, / a mighty shield and strong support, / a shelter from scorching wind and a shade from noonday sun, / a guard against stumbling and a help against falling."
- Psalm 46 // "God is our refuge and strength, / a very present help in trouble. . . . Be still, and know that I am God!"
- Psalm 16 // "Protect me, O God, for in you I take refuge."

- Psalm 62:1–2, 6–9 // "For God alone my soul waits in silence; / from him comes my salvation; He alone is my rock and my salvation, / my fortress; I shall never be shaken."
- Ephesians 3:14–21 // "I pray that . . . Christ may dwell in your hearts through faith, as you are being rooted and grounded in love."

10

We Are Never Alone

I leaned my head back on the lumpy hospital pillow as I stretched out on a makeshift bed that was next to my granddad's hospital bed. Even though I was exhausted, I knew sleep would not come. I tried to close my eyes, but the vigil I kept by his bedside won over the sleep I knew I needed. Hours earlier, they had moved Boppy from ICU into a regular room. Within minutes of his arriving in the new room, his speech changed drastically, the left side of his face drooped, and he was slurring his words. It was brought to the nurse's attention, and immediately a team of people rushed in and rolled Boppy out for an emergency CT scan. He was back in his room now, and we were awaiting the results. My worry was that it was a stroke or irrevocable damage from the tumor removal. One of the night nurses, not knowing the results of the CT scan, had come in and said, "It is important to keep an eye on him tonight." So, here I was, keeping vigil at his bedside.

I watched Boppy breathe. The darkness of the hospital room and the sounds of the various apparatuses and monitors made it feel as if they were my only companions. I watched my granddad's chest rise and fall, rise and fall, rise and fall. Watching him breathe, I thought of my children. How often had I stood over their cribs watching the rise and fall of their chests and breathing a sigh of relief every time another breath came. My motherly heart ached to be with them now. I longed for a few minutes to put aside this vigil I was keeping over my grand-dad and surround myself with my children's laughter and issues. How I longed to be home refereeing Lego-share fights or "she looked at me funny" spats. What I would not have given to have Chris, my best friend, my support, and my husband, by my side to keep vigil with me and carry some of the watch that night. Utter despair and confusion set in as I tried to process all the emotions stirring, including my love for my grandfather, my love for my children and husband. The ache to be with all of them and the worry for what was happening to my granddad swallowed me.

I felt utterly alone. I felt hopeless. I felt afraid.

Out of the depth of my despair and crying out for help, a phrase came into my mind and heart: *God is here.* Its entrance paused my anguish momentarily. Something about this phrase felt true and trusted. The fleeting respite passed, and I felt myself crying out internally again about how alone I felt. *God is here.* These three words returned and again paused my turmoil as my heart captured and savored them. *God is here. God is here. God is here.*

These words began to build momentum, a resounding drum beating out one of God's promises in my heart. *God is here. God is here. God is here.* As the rhythm of the words steadied me, I could feel the cloud of loneliness and despair begin to dissipate. I took a deep breath and remembered one of the things I share with people on retreats and in talks: the inner chapel. The place where God resides within each of us. The safe space in each of us. The sanctuary within, where God is always present.

I chuckled to think of the number of times I have reminded people that they are never alone, that God is always with them. And yet, when I was faced with a challenging, painful moment, I forgot the very thing I remind people to cling to.

As the understanding of this washed over me, I released a deep breath that I didn't even realize I was holding. I let my head fall further back into my pillow and closed my eyes and allowed myself to enter the sacred space within. Peace filled me as I remembered that I am never alone and that God is always with me, even as I kept watch over my grandfather. The vigil became easier as I embraced one of God's promises—that I was not alone. My hope increased even more as I remembered that neither was Boppy. God was within him, too.

The comfort of this steady presence in both our lives brought deep peace. I knew we were both going to be okay no matter what the night held, because God was there. I could feel the doors of my inner chapel opening further to welcome me. As I entered this safe space that felt as familiar and comfortable as a favorite pair of worn blue jeans, I knew that I could pour out my heart to God. I did just that.

One of the final memories I have of that night is thanking God as I went to sleep that someone had told me long ago that the inner chapel existed. Even though I was not at Mass, or in a church, God was with me.

You are not alone either.

When have you felt utterly alone? Have you ever felt that the weight of loneliness might crush you? I can think of other times besides that night in the ICU when I experienced extreme loneliness.

- The day my husband returned to work and I was alone for the first time with our week-old son. I felt the responsibility of caring for God's beautiful gift to us—and I felt uncertainty about how to live out motherhood. Sheer panic set in for a few minutes, as I understood the reality that I was the only adult around to care for this infant.

- When we uprooted our lives in Louisiana and moved away from our hometown for the first time to a new city where we knew no one. The loneliness that year almost swallowed me at times as I desperately yearned for friendships and a community.
- Times in the middle of the night when I cannot sleep and I am tossing and turning about a concern. Sometimes, the silence of the night makes me feel as if I am holding my concern solo.
- When I am celebrating a major moment of joy and I feel that no one understands the magnitude of what this joyous occasion means to me.
- When the weight of what I am holding feels brutally heavy and I feel that no one around me notices the load I am carrying.

What about you? When have you experienced utter loneliness? When have you felt the despair of feeling alone?

When moments like these hit, they can be hard to walk through. It seems, though, that in these moments we touch our yearning for relationships. When we look around us and see no one physically there or we feel that people do not understand what's happening to us, it can stir deep feelings of loneliness.

Embracing God's gift of the inner chapel helps me tremendously when I experience loneliness. By visiting it each day for almost two decades, I believe I am finally beginning to understand the words in the Gospel of John where Jesus promises us the Advocate—the Holy Spirit—and promises us we will never be alone: "I will not leave you orphaned" (John 14:18). When I think of these words and repeat them to myself, something inside shifts and brings a bit of light into the dark loneliness. Remembering that God promises to be with me and that I am never alone is deeply comforting. When I first began to understand this years ago, it caused a life-altering shift, one I am still trying to deepen and believe in more.

It comforts me to know that I am not left on my own to figure out things. I am not alone in growing in my relationship with God. I am not alone in making any decisions. I am not alone in walking through joys or heartbreaking sorrow.

God is always with me, residing in that chapel I carry with me wherever I go. God's friendship and presence are unshakable gifts of companionship and give me reason to hope. I am never alone, because God is with me. I know and believe this in my bones because of my own experience of God's presence and also from the hours and hours of listening to people's prayer experiences in spiritual direction.

In a time when we often face growing isolation and loneliness, it is a relief to know that we are never alone. God is not simply always with us; God is also not leaving us on our own to figure things out. The Holy Spirit is our advocate, given to us, and "will teach [us] everything" (John 14:26). As we are reminded in Romans 8:26, the Holy Spirit groans on our behalf, comes to aid us in our weakness, and intercedes for us when we do not know how to pray.

What comfort to know that

- when we seek to grow in a relationship with God, the Holy Spirit is working with us in our steps forward.
- when we are feeling weak, the Holy Spirit supports our efforts to overcome temptation.
- when we do not know the words to pray, the Holy Spirit is praying with us and for us.

Because each of us has an inner chapel, we can meet God there at any time. This is true regardless of where we are, what we're doing, what we are facing, or what is happening around us. We believe in the Incarnation: God became flesh and made his dwelling among us. *Emmanuel* means "God with us."

I believe much of our faith journey is learning to believe and trust the Good News of our faith. One piece of this Good News is that we are never alone! We can be brave and persistent and speak this truth to ourselves over and over again. Take comfort in this promise of God, my dear brothers and sisters in Christ, for we are not, and never will be, alone.

Let's lean in to this good news so we can believe the promise of God that we are not orphaned and that God will be with us always. And as the Scriptures urge us, this Good News is not just for us to keep to ourselves but also for us to share boldly and freely with others.

The Chapel Moves with Us!

Because there is an inner chapel within us, at any point in our day we have a sacred space where we can pause for prayer. If we apply St. Ignatius's wisdom of preparing the night before for the next day's prayer, we can intentionally come to this space—even when we are on the go. Taking with us our desire to grow in our relationship with God and the gift of the inner chapel, our time for prayer can occur in the moments of pause, travel, and waiting that are part of our weekly schedules. Here are a few examples.

Years ago, there was a gap of about thirty minutes between my youngest child's carpool line and my older children's carpool line. I found myself having twenty to thirty minutes of waiting and stillness as my youngest fell asleep during the commute and as I waited in line for my older two. I realized that this was built-in daily prayer time. I began to prepare for this prayer time by keeping in my car my journal, a Bible, and other prayer materials. Each day, I would turn the radio off and go to my inner chapel in that carpool line with my youngest napping in her car seat.

I've also watched my directees incorporate prayer into their daily, on-the-go lives.

- A mother of three found time to go to her inner chapel as she waited during her preschool daughter's dance class. She brought her journal with her, and this became a sacred time of reviewing her week of prayer.
- A father of a boy in middle school used his son's multiple baseball practices each week as a time to pray.
- A working professional used her time driving to work to listen to a daily reflection on the day's Gospel reading.
- A schoolteacher would begin her break by going to her inner chapel and reading the daily Scripture reflection.

These are just a handful of examples of how I witness people tap into sacred space and the gift of the chapel that moves with us even when life is busy.

Maybe you understand this already, or maybe this is new for you. Maybe you need to rediscover this aspect of the Good News—that you are not alone. Let me offer a tool that helps me daily increase my faith that God is with me and that I am never alone.

The *Examen*

So often people ask me, "How do I know if I encountered God or God encountered me?" Or some might ask what God looks like. While it would be amazing if the person of Jesus were walking around on this planet, we were given the gift of the Holy Spirit to help us grow in awareness of God with us.

In Isaiah 11:1–3 we read a prophetic text about the promise of the Messiah. This Scripture tells us what the spirit of the Lord will look like.

A shoot shall come out from the stump of Jesse, / and a branch shall grow out of his roots. / The spirit of the LORD shall rest on him, / the spirit of wisdom and of understanding, / the spirit of counsel and might, / the spirit of knowledge and the fear of the LORD. / His delight shall be in the fear of the LORD. / He shall not judge by what his eyes see, / or decide by what his ears hear.

The prophet Isaiah tells us that God with us (Emmanuel) looks like a spirit of wisdom and understanding, of knowledge, and of fear of the Lord. While this is pointing to the coming of Jesus, it reminds us of what God's presence still looks like today.

In Galatians 5:22, we get a clearer description of what the Holy Spirit looks like.

In contrast, the fruit of the Spirit is love, joy, peace, patience, kindness, generosity, faithfulness, gentleness, and self-control.

In our day-to-day lives, we can identify where we experienced love, joy, peace, patience, kindness, generosity, faithfulness, gentleness, and self-control. It reminds me, too, of 2 Corinthians 3:17, which says, "Where the Spirit of the Lord is, there is freedom."

Galatians 5:19 also reminds us of what the works of the flesh look like.

Now the works of the flesh are obvious: fornication, impurity, licentiousness, idolatry, sorcery, enmities, strife, jealousy, anger, quarrels, dissensions, factions, envy, drunkenness, carousing, and things like these. I am warning you, as I warned you before: those who do such things will not inherit the kingdom of God.

The prayer tool called the *examen*, can help us each day bring the past twenty-four hours before God to reflect on where we experienced the fruit of the Spirit and where we experienced the opposite.

What Is the *Examen*?

The *examen* is attributed to St. Ignatius. Ignatius's own experience taught him the value of reviewing his day with God's help. The *examen* helps us name God at work in our day, and it also helps us pay attention to where we messed up and did not help bring the fruit of the Spirit into our lives or the lives of others.

The *examen* is simply a review of the past twenty-four hours. We bring the day before God, which means we never run out of material for prayer.

Because the *examen* requires no prayer material other than the activities of our day and the material of our lives, we can pray the *examen* at any time and anywhere. This prayer tool goes where we go.

We can walk through the five steps of the *examen* in prayer in all kinds of places. Here are a few examples (from my own life and from the lives of those who come to me for spiritual direction) of how people incorporate this daily discipline of reviewing the day with God's help.

- While taking a bath or shower
- On a run or walk
- When driving a car
- As part of normal daily prayer
- In bed before falling asleep
- In the middle of a workday, sitting at a desk or on a bench outside

Whenever and wherever God invites you to pause for ten minutes to pray the *examen*, I invite you to go to your inner chapel now and give the *examen* a try.

LET'S GO TO THE INNER CHAPEL

Praying the Examen

1. Invite the Holy Spirit to help you see your day as God sees it.
2. Be thankful. Name the gifts of your day and thank God for them.
3. Notice God's presence. Where did you feel an increase of faith, hope, and love?
4. Notice where you felt what seemed like a lack of God's presence. Where did you feel a decrease of faith, hope, and love? Why?
5. Look to the future. Ask God for the grace you need in the day ahead. Close with an Our Father.

This prayer tool is one I use frequently when I go to my inner chapel. I invite you now to go to your inner chapel and give this prayer a try. I've included several Scripture passages to pray with that will help you remember that we are not alone.

Embracing the Promises of God

These Scriptures can encourage you as you read them and pray with them.

- John 14:18 // "I will not leave you."
- Isaiah 43 // "I will be with you."
- Matthew 28:16–20 // The commissioning of the disciples

11

We Belong to Someone

Growing up and throughout the high-school years, I felt that I belonged. There were communities around me: family, church, friends, and school. My community felt large and expansive, spreading to extended family and long family friendships. It felt good to belong. I always knew where I belonged, who my people were, and what my sense of purpose was.

One disconcerting thing that began during my junior and senior years of high school and only amplified as I began college was the awakening of my desire for a relationship with God. It may seem odd to use the word *disconcerting* about a faith journey, but that's what it felt like a bit to me. As I began responding to God's pursuit of me, everything I once knew and understood didn't make sense anymore. Old ways of doing things. Old habits. Friendships and even relationships with family members suddenly seemed different. I was looking at the world through a whole new lens, and it left me feeling very out of place. Old groups I belonged to and goals I used to care about changed. While in high school my goals were to work hard, push myself, earn good grades, and receive recognition, something internally was shifting that left me clueless as to my purpose and my way.

During the summer between my senior year of high school and freshman year of college, I experienced the first death of a friend, a terminal diagnosis of another, and the move from my home to a large university. These changes of loss and transition made it seem that the world as I knew it had been pulled out from under me, and I was reeling to find my place and to redefine home. What once felt like a stable place of belonging no longer felt like home.

These changes, along with my diving deeper into my faith, were creating inner turmoil for me. Not even family members understood my newly invigorated and passionate faith. If I may be honest, when I look back at myself in those early years of discovering a personal relationship with God, I was probably obnoxious to some people. It was most likely a startling and drastic change for them, as it was for me. A relationship with God changes you; it changed me, but also my relationships. I couldn't name it then, but now, twenty years later, I can identify it as part of the "cost of discipleship." My newfound faith cost me some friendships and caused strained relationships with some family members.

During the first years of college, I struggled to belong despite my efforts of "being involved" in college groups and activities. The safety and security of belonging that I'd known growing up were either shifting or no longer there. Even my sense of belief and understanding of God did not make sense anymore.

In those years of turmoil, I found my way with God's help, both in prayer and in finding a community of people who understood me—people such as the youth office staff at the Diocese of Baton Rouge, which brought into my life an army of people who cared about their faith lives. These people cared for me and equipped me with tools of faith to help with my prayer and also with answering my call—discerning what God wanted me to do with my life. I was helped by people such as Sr. Ily, who believed that even though I was young, I was worthy of her time to accompany me. People such as my husband, Chris, who also had discovered his faith in late high school and early college. These people helped me find my way through that first season of feeling as if I did not belong.

I know that for some of you reading this, your first time of not belonging was at a younger age in elementary, junior high, or high school. Others of you faced this feeling later, in adulthood. I imagine that some of you reading this right now might be struggling at this moment to feel as if you belong.

What I've come to discover over the past two decades is that this sense of not belonging can develop in many ways.

Not Belonging in a Community

Being an outsider is hard. I've learned this from moving to different cities and states. It's hard leaving a community where you know people and you are known and entering one where others don't know you and you don't know them. I can remember that feeling of wondering *Where in the heck do we belong now?* when we moved from Louisiana for the first time. I can remember watching the last family member who had helped us move drive away from our new home in Georgia. I stood there bawling and overwhelmed with emotions and questions: *Where do I belong now? Where is my home?* This experience repeated when we resettled from Georgia to Texas and then from Texas back home to Louisiana. Each time, we left behind a place of familiarity.

Our communities shift for other reasons as we change churches, our children change schools, we or our spouses change jobs, and so on. Such shifts in community can leave us feeling alone and also isolated—that is, not belonging. Sometimes, despite our best efforts to reach out and meet new people, we are met with coldness, or closedness because tight-knit, life-long groups of friends or colleagues are so comfortable in their groups that there is no need to make room for a newcomer. I experienced that before and, sadly, I have watched my children experience this, too, in our relocations and moves.

I know I am not the only one who has experienced this; I have listened to a multitude of stories from people not knowing where they belong anymore because of a shift in their community. Even more painful sometimes is when there is a shift in our families.

Not Belonging in Our Families

Some of the greatest angst for me and others (judging from the many stories people have told me), is the angst that comes from shifts in a family system. While our hope for our families is that they are loving, welcoming, and secure, often our brokenness as human beings can host a world of hurt for the ones we love the most. Families are ripped apart for all sorts of reasons: addiction, divorce, death, betrayal, abuse. People are ostracized from their families for their beliefs, their sexuality, their political views, and so much more. Spouses hurt each other. Parents hurt their children. Children hurt their parents. When our place where we learned security and worth is broken, we can feel that we are outside or somehow left apart from what used to feel like home but does so no longer.

Many share with me in spiritual direction also how their family of origin perhaps did not provide an environment that felt secure, safe, or like a place of belonging from the beginning. This happens in families that struggle with poverty, with family members who are addicted or mentally ill, and with patterns of verbal, physical, or sexual abuse. Changing physical homes, shifting relationships, and living on the edge can have a profound impact on who we are and how we see ourselves. Such pain and estrangement can leave us feeling that we never belong anywhere or to anyone.

As a mother and a wife, it is not easy to acknowledge the reality that out of my humanness I might hurt the ones I love the most and the ones who are closest to me, namely my husband and children. While we strive to offer an environment of love, hope, and belonging in our family, there is a good chance that at some point even those in my home will have a moment of feeling that they don't belong. There is nothing that shows me my need for God more than naming this reality. I need God to help me love my loved ones well.

Not Belonging in Our Calling

I have spent much of the past twenty years trying to work through the tension of knowing what God calls me to and not always feeling welcome among colleagues to pursue my calling because of my young age and, at times, my gender. Honestly, I could write a whole book about this journey, and one day I might. But it is a very lonely feeling to know that God has called you to something and to have people around you not understand it or not make you feel welcome to enact what you feel God calling you to.

Sometimes I listen to great pain from others who strongly feel God calling them to use their gifts in a specific way. The call is clear, and yet sometimes even their own churches do not make them feel welcome to respond to their calls or allow them to share their gifts. What do people do when they know they are called to something and their own communities do not help them answer the call?

I guess we shouldn't be surprised by this; even Jesus was rejected by his hometown crowd when he stood up in the synagogue and unrolled the scroll to announce his call and mission:

When they heard this, all in the synagogue were filled with rage They got up, drove him out of the town, and led him to the brow of the hill on which their town was built, so that they might hurl him off the cliff. (Luke 4:28–29)

Jesus might be showing us what it really means to follow God, that it will require loving God over all others in our lives, even our families. I can remember so many times hearing the Gospel passages about Jesus seeming to pick God over his loved ones and feeling very perplexed and confused, such as the time Mary and Joseph could not find him anywhere and searched for him for three days before finding him in the temple.

Mary asks him, "Child, why have you treated us like this? Your father and I have been searching for you in great anxiety." He said to them, "Why were you searching for me? Didn't you know that I must be in my Father's house?" (Luke 2:48–49). Even the tiny glimpse we get of Jesus during his youth shows us that he already had an understanding of whom he belonged to the most.

Later we see more startling examples of Jesus belonging to those who do the will of his Father more than anyone else:

> While [Jesus] was still speaking to the crowds, his mother and his brothers were standing outside, wanting to speak to him. Someone told him, "Look, your mother and your brothers are standing outside, wanting to speak to you." But to the one who had told him this, Jesus replied, "Who is my mother, and who are my brothers?" And pointing to his disciples, he said, "Here are my mother and my brothers! For whoever does the will of my Father in heaven is my brother and sister and mother." (Matthew 12:46–50)

In the Gospel of Mark, Jesus' family members hear about him living his calling, and it says they went to take charge of him, "for people were saying, 'He has gone out of his mind'" (Mark 3:20–21). Jesus' family did not understand who he was or what God had called him to. In Luke's Gospel, we read of Jesus saying, "Whoever comes to me and does not hate father and mother, wife and children, brothers and sisters, yes, and even life itself, cannot be my disciple. Whoever does not carry the cross and follow me cannot be my disciple" (Luke 14:25–27).

The best explanation I read of this was in a homily by St. Augustine in which he stated that what God is asking of us is to love God more than anyone else in our lives, even our closest loved ones. Jesus knew God called him to a mission and to love God more than anyone, even his parents, Mary and Joseph. Despite not always belonging or being understood, Jesus clung to the solid ground that his relationship with God gave him. Belonging to God enabled Jesus to overcome the loss of friendships, community, and support in his own hometown. Belonging to God helped him overcome even death on the cross.

Solid Ground

The solid ground that Jesus had in belonging to God is our solid ground also. One thing has remained steady for me throughout the years, and it is only in the past few years that I have come to understand, in a whole new way, the promise of God that we belong to someone.

This belief in the value of visiting our inner chapels is not superficial or fluffy self-help. The daily discipline of pausing to be still and go to my inner chapel has saved me many times from utter despair or loneliness. It has given me solid footing even when loved ones hurt me or I hurt them. The inner chapel offers the great gift of stillness and silence. But the even greater gift is that when I enter the silence, I am going to be with Someone—Someone to whom I belong.

There is deep comfort in knowing that I belong to God, that I am known by God, and that I know God. Even when relationships change around me, I still belong to God. When life shifts and my communities change, one thing always remains: I belong to Someone who knows me and loves me deeply.

I want to share with you a profound moment of prayer that to this day offers comfort and security to me. A couple years ago, I entered my annual silent retreat at Eastern Point Retreat House in Gloucester, Massachuesetts with a long season of transition behind me. My first book had come out earlier that year, and it was shifting my calls in many ways. I was struggling to find my footing and voice in knowing where I belonged.

On a much more personal level, my grandfather was declining. Two days before I left to make this silent retreat, he had slipped and ended up in the ER again in Baton Rouge. While he was there, we learned that his incision from previous surgeries was still not healing properly, and it continued to allow air to enter his brain, causing an air pocket to push on parts of his brain, which resulted in almost complete paralysis of his left side at times. At around ten in the evening they transferred him via ambulance from the Baton Rouge ER to the hospital in New Orleans for surgery early the next morning, Halloween.

That night I stayed with Boppy at the hospital. As we lay in the dark, he in his bed and I on the cot in the room, he suddenly broke the silence: "Becksa, you awake?" Nowhere close to being able to fall asleep after the adrenaline of the evening, he began a long conversation about his hopes, his fears, his final preparations. He asked profound questions about death amid sharing the depth of his love and gratitude for his life and loved ones. His honesty and trust in what he shared stirred a complexity of emotions in me. Deep love for him and gratitude for his trust to share. Deep sadness as we talked about the reality of his death. This conversation, even with its complexity, reminded me of how safe I had always felt with him. How I knew I belonged to him. I knew him. I was known to him. I belonged.

The next morning, we woke with only a few hours of sleep behind us. Thankfully, he had an easy surgery; they cleaned the wound and stitched him back up. The doctors shared with us the ongoing concern of the decline they saw in the wound condition, in his weight loss, and in his weakening health. Even within those moments of his recovery, he remembered important details of my life. At one moment, he called me over to his bedside and said, "Becksa, I know your retreat starts tomorrow. You have to go. It's always been your special time with God. I also know tonight is Halloween. You go home to your kids tonight. I'll be okay. Other family members and friends are here. I already told them you need to go home for trick or treat and your retreat."

Without my speaking my inner turmoil and wrestling about being in two places at once, Boppy knew what was in my heart: the struggle of wanting to be with all the people I love at once, both with him and my family. Also, knowing the gift of my long time with God on retreat in helping me stay grounded in life's responsibilities. After a few more conversations with him, with Chris, and other family members, I headed home.

As I drove the hour back to Baton Rouge to make it home in time for trick or treating that night, the silence in the car enveloped me. As it did, I began talking to God about all that had transpired in the past twenty-four hours: the sudden ER trip after Boppy's fall, the transfer of hospital in the middle of the night, our conversation, my grandfather's surgery, and his blessing. My tears held a mix of gratitude, joy, and deep sadness as the reality hit of what was coming my way soon. I was going to lose one of the people I always belonged to and who always made me feel I belonged.

It was in this reality that I began my silent retreat the next day. The sadness of his diagnosis hit me like a ton of bricks as I allowed myself to enter the silence deeper and deeper. I cried out to God to save him, to heal him. I also cried out for God to ready him and all of us for what was coming. My deepest cries were ones of sadness and sorrow at losing this man I loved.

On that retreat, I found myself one night praying with the Scripture of the woman at the well in the Gospel of John. This has long been a well-loved passage of mine, and I sat in the Mary chapel at the retreat house praying with this Scripture again. After rereading it, I closed my eyes and entered my inner chapel. I began to call the scene of this Scripture into my mind. I pictured the well and what it looked like. I saw Jesus sitting at the well. As I placed myself in the scene, as Ignatian contemplation invites us to do, I stood off in the distance with someone, looking at Jesus and the well. I realized the person standing with me was Mary. Mary invited me to walk to the well with her. In my mind, I could see us shoulder to shoulder, going to her son. As we walked, we talked about all I was feeling. The joy, the gratitude, and the impending loss. Mary listened and comforted. As our journey to the well ended, we were suddenly standing in front of Jesus. I could feel his loving eyes staring right at me before I was able to lock my eyes with his. When I was able to, he just held my gaze in the most loving way for a long time. Then, he turned to his mother and said words that reminded me of the words asked of Chris and me at each of our kids' baptisms: "Woman, what name do you give this child?" Mary responded, "Christ-light bearer." Jesus then dipped his hand in the well and with his wet fingers marked me with the sign of the cross on my forehead. As he did, he said, "I claim you as my own." Then he invited his mother to do the same. Mary then dipped her hand into the well and turned to me and said, "I claim you as my daughter. You are mine." I wept in my imagination and in real time and place. I was overtaken, lovingly, by the powerful presence of belonging—of being so deeply loved and cared for, of being known.

I have replayed this moment of prayer in my mind hundreds of times, savoring the gift and grace of it. It is a moment and prayer that profoundly changed me. It was a deep assurance that no matter what change or loss has happened or what change or loss *might* happen, I will always belong to someone. That gives me deep comfort and confidence that I find difficult to articulate here.

What I want to tell you, though, is that this promise of God is not only for me. And while it came to me most clearly that night on my silent retreat, it is a promise of God that was given to me long before that night. It is a promise of God that is available to you also. You belong to Someone. You belong to God.

This is not just the promise of not being alone but that we belong to someone in an intimate way. That someone loves and cares for us and knows us and wants to be known by us. That is the deepest longing of our human hearts that I encounter . . . to belong not only somewhere but also to Someone.

Whom Do We Belong To?

We belong to God, to Jesus, to the Holy Spirit. We belong to Mary and to the communion of saints. We belong to all the holy men and women who have gone before us. Our belonging comes in these forms.

First and foremost, we belong to God because we were created and formed by God. Our very existence comes out of a creative act of love by God who cared deeply enough about us to form us in a unique, unrepeatable way. There is no one, not one other person in this world, who is like you or me. We belong to God, our creator.

Second, we are named and claimed by God. Yes, we are given our names by our parents and those who raise us, but we are also named and claimed by God in our relationship with God. Many times, the Scriptures proclaim, "You will be my people, and I will be your God."

Third, we are chosen and called. God chose us to be in relationship with God. God chooses us as God's people. God calls us not only into relationship with God but also to use our gifts and calls in a unique way. On days when I am close to forgetting this promise, I repeat these words like a mantra:

> I am created and formed, named and claimed, chosen and called.
> I am created and formed, named and claimed, chosen and called.
> I am created and formed, named and claimed, chosen and called.

These words remind me that I belong. Maybe they will help you also to know that you are created and formed, named and claimed, chosen and called by God. You are not alone. You belong to God.

LET'S GO TO THE INNER CHAPEL

Created and Formed

"It was you who formed me in my inward parts; / you knit me together in my mother's womb" (Psalm 139:13).

You are a unique creation—unrepeatable. Pause and reflect on the way God created you and formed you before you were aware of your own choice.

- What are some characteristics of my creation that came to me before I had the ability to choose them—for example, my parents? My gender? The place I was born? Where I lived when I was younger? Physical characteristics? Siblings? Extended family? Culture I was born into?

- What characteristics have I inherited from my parents, extended family, or family of origin? Which characteristics do I like? Which characteristics do I perhaps not prefer?

- What parts of my original family dynamics assisted in my growth? Which parts of my original family dynamics have hindered my growth?

- What are my personal characteristics and qualities that were born in me before I was aware of my own choice? (For example: the language I speak, habits, sexual orientation, cultural norms)

Named and Claimed

"I have called you by name, you are mine" (Isaiah 43:1).

Go to your inner chapel. Imagine that you are the one being brought to the well to be claimed by Jesus. Imagine Jesus marking you with the sign of the cross, claiming you as his own. What name does he give you? What does it feel like to be named and claimed by Jesus?

In what other moments of your life can you remember being claimed by Jesus?

Chosen and Called

"You did not choose me but I chose you. And I appointed you to go and bear fruit, fruit that will last, so that the Father will give you whatever you ask him in my name" (John 15:16).

Go to your inner chapel. Invite the Holy Spirit to help you remember moments in your life when God chose you and called you.

What moments can you recall being chosen and called by God? When were you called into relationship initially? What times did God invite you deeper into relationship? When did God call you to use your gifts to bear fruit for others?

Embracing the Promises of God

These Scriptures can encourage you as you read them and pray with them.

- Galatians 3:22–29 // "In Christ Jesus you are children of God through faith. . . . If you belong to Christ."
- Psalm 100 // "Know that the LORD is God . . . and we are his; we are his people."
- Ephesians 2:13–15 // "But now in Christ Jesus you who once were far off have been brought near by the blood of Christ."
- John 15:4 // "Abide in me as I abide in you."

12

We Are Loved—Unconditionally

There were seven stepping-stones that separated our home from my grandparents' home. Almost every day as a child, I skipped or hopped across these stones to make my way to their carport door. With excitement I would fling open the screen door and knock our special knock, "tat-tat-a-tat-tat," letting them know it was one of the grandchildren at the door. I always waited eagerly to see who would get to the door first, my grandmother or my grandfather. The sound of the doorknob beginning to turn only made my excitement build. Then the crescendo moment of the door flying open to see the smiling face of one of my grandparents. No matter who it was behind the door, there was a unique welcome when the door flew open. One that reminded me of the way Isaiah 43 writes about how God calls us by name. "Hey, Becky-D!" if it was my grandmother or "Hey, Becksa!" if it was my grandfather. From the second the greeting hit my ears, I could feel that deep sense of love welling up.

Once inside, the warmth of their home, the smells of Grandmother's cooking, and their hospitality made me feel welcomed and deeply loved. Often I would hop onto one of their brown barstools at the white Formica counter speckled with gold flakes, eagerly hoping that one of them would offer me a treat. Rarely did they disappoint! It might be one of my grandmother's pralines or her favorite iced oatmeal cookies or veggies with Hidden Valley Ranch Dip. If Granddad was around, he might splurge and offer a Sprite float, made in my favorite pink cup, with Blue Bell vanilla ice cream. While I sipped and snacked, they would shower attention on me through their eagerness to listen to my stories and find out about what was going on in my life.

This ritual continued through high school, and it was then that I found the comfort of their white couch with green stripes and pink roses. My visits evolved from childish hopes for treats to yearning for time to talk to them and listen to their wisdom, advice, and stories. They listened to my dating woes, my stresses in school, and my hopes and dreams. Throughout high school, their support went beyond the walls of their home as they showed up at cross-country races, track meets, and every milestone of my high school career.

College, with all its newness, transitions, and losses, brought a deeper appreciation of the security I found when sitting on my grandparents' couch. I always felt heard and listened to when I sat there and told them about my life. I sought their advice and wisdom more and more as I made decisions about majors, dating, and career. They always took the time to listen to and hear every detail of what I shared. I can remember the day I told my grandmother that my now husband, Chris, had asked me out on a "non-date" for Valentine's Day. Knowing well enough that I had mentioned his name before, she cackled with laughter at this idea of a "non-date" and said, "Becky-D, I sure hope you enjoy your date with Chris!" Wise as she was because she knew me so intimately, she reminded us of this "non-date" when we were all at the rehearsal dinner for our wedding.

The morning of our wedding, I walked across those seven stepping-stones again and sat and drank coffee with them before getting ready and walking down the aisle to begin my new life with Chris. As Chris entered the scene and became part of our family, they welcomed and loved him as they had always loved me: fully. The way they loved him opened him to receive and give love in a whole new way.

As our family grew, I watched my experience of being their young granddaughter repeat through the eyes of my children. Because we lived across town—and later across the country—there were no stepping-stones for my children to cross to see their great-grandparents. But they experienced the same excitement I had felt when opening the screen door and doing our special knock, "tat-tat-a-tat-tat." Their joy and excitement matched the joy and excitement of my grandparents seeing their great-grandchildren. My grandparents created special names for them just as they did for me growing up. Our son: "Brady-buster." Our middle daughter: "Abby-girl." Our younger daughter: "Mer-Mer."

My grandparents let me know I was deeply loved. They let Chris know he was deeply loved. They let each of my children know they were deeply loved. Their love for me prepared me to open my life to God's love.

Who Taught Jesus He Was Lovable?

Have you ever thought about how Jesus came to understand he was lovable? Or have you ever wondered how Jesus learned how to love? These are two questions I've pondered quite often.

It's easy to think that Jesus popped out of Mary's womb understanding all the mysteries of the world, including the fact that he was fully loved by God. If we think like this, though, we underestimate the fact that Jesus was human—fully human. Jesus entered humanity so that we can understand the way to live fully loved. This means that Jesus grew into his understanding of God's love for him just as we do.

In his address at the Prayer Vigil on September 26, 2015, at the World Meeting of Families, Pope Francis said, "And where did he (God) send his Son? To a palace, to a city, to an office building? He sent him to a family. God came into the world in a family." Jesus, like us, learned that he was lovable through the concrete gestures of holiness that his parents, Mary and Joseph, offered him: the basic acts of feeding him, clothing him, keeping him safe. While much is not written in Scriptures about Jesus' childhood, we get glimpses of the love his parents had for him in simple gestures.

- Mary wrapping him in swaddling clothes: Luke 2:7
- Shepherds coming to see the Christ child, and Mary reflecting on all these things in her heart: Luke 2:8–19
- Mary and Joseph taking Jesus to the temple to be circumcised and presented to their faith community: Luke 2:22–38
- Mary and Joseph journeying for a day, looking for Jesus before finding him in the temple: Luke 2:44–46

Given that Jesus was human, like each of us, every gesture of love, or as Pope Francis names them, "little gestures of holiness," helped Jesus know he was lovable. Each of these experiences of love given to him by his parents and his community opened his capacity to know that he was fully loved by God.

Who Taught Us That We Are Lovable?

Fr. Joe Tetlow, SJ, includes a prayer exercise called "Prayer on My Dossier" in his version of the *Spiritual Exercises*. A dossier is a collection of documents about a particular person or subject. He invites us to remember our lives and create a dossier. As we note each piece of data from our lives, we are invited to "raise [our] mind and heart to God [our] Maker, and praise and thank the Creator for this detail in my life history and in myself."[18]

Looking back over our life stories, can we name people who showed us that we have value or worth because of the concrete gestures of holiness they offered us?

- Meals provided by a parent or family member
- A loved one providing shelter for us when we were growing up
- A teacher investing a little extra time to help us understand a topic
- A coach or extracurricular teacher seeing a talent in us and having the courage to push us to use it to its fullest
- A significant other caring to hear about our day
- A friend showing up to celebrate a moment or be present during a difficult time

When I look back over my life, I can name many ways that I came to understand God's love for me through the concrete gestures of others.

What Opens Us to God's Love?

What would it take for you to accept that you are fully loved by God? For some of us, accepting this foundational understanding comes easy. For many others of us, this is one of the hardest things we will ever work through—not just knowing we are loved by God but also accepting it in our bones.

So often I wish that more were written about the years of Jesus' childhood, teens, and early adulthood. Don't you? I want a glimpse into his life to understand more about who his friends were, what his family life was like, and what he enjoyed doing in his spare time. Much of Jesus' "hidden years," as they are often called, can be deciphered only through studying the culture of the times.

---

18. Joseph A. Tetlow, SJ, *Choosing Christ in the World* (Saint Louis: The Institute for Jesuit Sources, 1999), 119.

The bulk of what we know about Jesus, though, comes through reading the Scriptures. In them we find some events in Jesus' life that can tell us something about how we come to accept God's love for us.

Jesus' Baptism

John the Baptist understood something about Jesus before many others did. He lets us in on this when Jesus approaches John to be baptized. John's response is, "I need to be baptized by you, and do you come to me?" (Matthew 3:14). He reluctantly agrees to baptize Jesus, and when he does, something profound happens. The sky opens and a dove descends over Jesus' head, and a voice says, "You are my Son, the Beloved; with you I am well pleased" (Mark 1:11).

Note that God is not telling people around him that Jesus is his beloved son, as he will do later at the Transfiguration ("This is my son, listen to him!"), but he is speaking directly to Jesus: "*You* are my beloved Son." God is affirming Jesus and Jesus' mission.

Doesn't this provide you some relief? That Jesus, God's son, was told these words? Maybe, just maybe, Jesus needed the same reminder of God's love for him that we need. He was fully human and grew into his call, just as we grow into our holiness. Those words spoken directly to Jesus strengthened his belief that he was fully loved by God—just as he was. Perhaps Jesus needed that same reminder to accept who he was: God's beloved Son. Perhaps Jesus needed a clear moment of consolation to help him accept who he was and what he was called to do.

What about Us?

Wouldn't it be amazing if the sky opened and a dove descended over our heads and God spoke those words aloud to us?

My guess is that this hasn't happened. However, I bet we can name events or moments that have opened our capacity to accept

God's love for us. Moments that provided a brief glimpse of us as people loved just as we are.

- Perhaps there was a moment in prayer when a word or phrase from Scripture spoke so directly to your heart that you knew God loved you.
- Or maybe a loved one served as a concrete answer to your prayer request, teaching you that God hears our prayers and has the power to answer them.
- Maybe you felt God's love for you when a friend came and sat with you in your mess, your suffering, your loss, or your pain, reminding you of the way God cares about our hurts.
- Or maybe the kindness of a stranger popped into your day that wasn't going so well.

We experience hundreds of little moments that open our capacity to accept that we are loved by God and to strengthen our belief that we are fully loved. When we've been wounded or hurt deeply, it may take a long time for us to trust the authentic experience of God's love for us.

Prayer

Prayer, prayer, prayer—I cannot reiterate enough the value of spending time with God. We can go to God's word, the Scriptures, and read them, pray with them, and listen to God's words of love and promises for us.

- Psalm 139 // "It was you who formed my inward parts; / you knit me together in my mother's womb. / I praise you, for I am fearfully and wonderfully made. / Wonderful are your works."
- Isaiah 43 // "I have called you by name, you are mine."

- Psalm 103:8 // "The LORD is merciful and gracious, / slow to anger and abounding in steadfast love."

When we hear these words repeatedly and over time, we begin to accept them as truth. We begin to believe that we are loved—fully loved—just as we are. I wonder how often God whispered this reminder to Jesus in the stillness of Jesus' own heart. I imagine it happened often, because this happens to us, too.

We can increase this desire to receive God's love by going to our inner chapel in prayer. First of all, we show up! The Holy Spirit supports us in showing up for prayer and in opening our hearts more and more to receive God's love for us.

Let's look at a few more ways we can increase our capacity to receive God's love for us.

Our desire for God. Our desire to be loved fully and wholeheartedly by God is one of the ways the Holy Spirit works within us. As Pope Francis reminds us, all we need is to desire to take the step: "The medicine is there, the healing is there—if only we take a small step toward God . . . or even just desire to take that step."[19] God will meet us in this desire to be loved and will increase that desire.

People who remind us we are lovable. Jesus surrounded himself with close friends. We, too, can seek to spend time with those who love us as we are. Receiving love from others opens us to receive love from God. Who are these people in your life?

The sacraments. I am a practicing Catholic, and I believe the sacraments offer us special graces that we often cannot fully understand or name when we receive them. The Eucharist reminds us each week of sacrificial love for God. Reconciliation reminds us of God's gift of

---

19. Pope Francis, *The Name of God Is Mercy: A Conversation with Andrea Tornielli* (New York: Penguin Random House, 2016), xviii.

mercy and healing. Anointing of the sick reminds us of God's care when our physical body weakens.

Spiritual direction. I've worked with a spiritual director for almost two decades. In my personal faith life, the gift of another person compassionately listening to me and helping me deepen my relationship with God has helped me increase my capacity to receive God's love. It's one of the many reasons I became a spiritual director, to help others come to know this also.

Retreats. If you have never made a silent retreat, I highly recommend considering it. This time away with God opens us in ways I cannot really put into words. Attending annual silent retreats has blessed me considerably. Like spiritual direction, retreats—and the gifts they have given me—have led me into the retreat ministry I do today. I want others to experience the gifts of God's profound love, mercy, and healing that can happen when we become still and listen.

The Challenge of Receiving God's Love

It is one thing to intellectually understand God's love for us, but it is a whole other thing to actually open our hearts to receive God's love. To be honest, sometimes the light and gift of God's love is so bright that we turn from it. The gift of love from God is so good, true, honest, and real that we are sometimes afraid to let ourselves receive it. It can feel too good to be true, so we sometimes doubt it or resist the love offered—love that is given freely and unconditionally, without our trying to earn it.

Our ability to reason can get in the way of receiving God's love because we can rationalize and list all the ways we are not worthy of God's love (or maybe we feel another person is not worthy of this freely given gift). Fortunately, God doesn't operate by our standards. We are loved as we are right now. Our task on this journey of faith is to increase our capacity to receive God's gift of love. Yet again, Jesus models the way for us to do this.

Jesus had a desire for a relationship with God even as a young boy when Mary and Joseph couldn't find him because he was in the temple: "After three days they found him in the temple, sitting among the teachers, listening to them and asking them questions" (Luke 2:46). Even at the age of twelve, Jesus had a desire for God.

Jesus nurtured this desire for God through prayer. As he grew into adulthood, we see that he was supported on his faith journey by his family and closest friends, his disciples. Jesus had moments such as his baptism that strengthened his relationship with God. In our own prayer, we will experience moments of encouragement and confirmation too. And if we forget this, let's recall the words of God spoken about Jesus at the Transfiguration to remind us of where to turn for an example: "This is my Son, the Beloved. . . . Listen to him!" (Matthew 17:5).

What Inhibits Us?

We sometimes get in our own way when it comes to accepting God's love for us. We listen to other voices that tell us we are not worthy to receive God's love. Voices speaking words such as

- You have to earn your worth.
- You have to get to a certain point on your faith journey before you are loved.
- Your worthiness of love is measured by what you own, what you do, or the amount of money you make.
- You are not qualified.

Sometimes we simply stop showing up in our relationship with God, and our hearts gradually close to God's love and mercy. At other times, our hearts grow hard and resistant because of something that happened to us that hurt so much that we do not trust to open our hearts to anyone, not even God.

The reality of our humanity is that we can close our hearts to God's love by giving in to everyday temptations that can cause us to make sinful choices. Perhaps we choose to live by the world's standards instead of God's, or maybe we harbor unforgiveness toward someone who has hurt us to the point that it begins to erode our trust in God's love and care for us. Or maybe we simply are closed off to the newness God is birthing within us because we are afraid of what we are being asked to do.

The work of our faith journey is to stay close to God and to live an examined life in which we are aware of what opens our hearts to receive God's love and also what closes our hearts to God's abundant gifts of love and mercy.

Jesus Models the Way

Just prior to going to the desert to fast for forty days and nights, Jesus was baptized and affirmed by God and strengthened for his mission. Jesus was then led into the desert, where he spent days in prayer, and as Scripture tells us, he was tempted by the devil and then ministered to by angels (Mark 1:12–13, Matthew 4:1–11, Luke 4:1–13).

Jesus' time in the desert shows us two important insights about overcoming things that can close us off from God's love and mercy. First, time with God in prayer, in silence, and in solitude strengthens us and opens us to what God has for us. Second, God helps us overcome temptations and anything else that threatens to close our hearts. Jesus stayed close to his Father.

Just as we can name who taught us we were lovable, we can probably also recall moments that made us pause and question if we are worthy of God's love. I invite you now to recall and remember moments that made you close your heart to God's love.

God's Ongoing Creation and Love

It is important for us to look at where we opened to God's love and also where we might feel closed to receiving God's love because God continues to create us moment by moment. God is loving us through the movements of openness and resistance.

God loves us through the moments we are proud of and the ones we are ashamed of. God loves us through the moments we overcome temptation and the ones we succumb to temptation. God loves us in all the moments that remind us we are lovable and those moments that make us feel unlovable.

God is always with us, loving us, tending to us moment by moment. We are never a finished product but an ongoing creation that the Creator continues to shape and mold.

Fr. Joe Tetlow, SJ, in his book *Making Choices in Christ*, reminds us of how God loves us in the here and now.

> You are who God wants you to be. God loves you as you are—not as you might be or could be. God loves you because you are who you are, for God is making you who you are. When you know this, you have accepted the most intimate relationship with God that a busy life allows, a relationship that fills all things.[20]

This is the foundation of everything regarding our faith: the depth to which we are loved by God. The ends of the earth that God will go to to love us. This is the most comforting promise of God that I can fathom: the depth of God's love for us.

The older my children get, the more I realize the urgency I feel to pass on the understanding that they are unconditionally loved by God. This desire stems from my motherly hope that they understand

---

20. Joseph A. Tetlow, SJ, *Making Choices in Christ: Foundations of Ignatian Spirituality* (Chicago: Loyola Press, 2008), 15.

- that they are embraced by God's love, which is greater and deeper than anything I can offer them.
- that God's love is transforming. As much as I love my children, I know that because of my humanity there will be times that I mess up and my offer of love to them falls short in some way.
- that the love of God is what gives them their value and worth. Nothing else and no one else can give them this.
- that they are loved profoundly, deeply, and unconditionally just as they are *right now*.
- that the love given to them by God is freely given and unearned.

What I know from my own life and from witnessing others grow in their relationship with God through spiritual direction is that something profound happens when a person opens to the unconditional love of God. I am convinced that we will never fully understand the magnitude of God's love, but I think much of our faith journey is trying to open ourselves, every day, a little bit more, to God's transforming love.

I feel as if I am witnessing a miracle when someone opens to this promise of God, that they are unconditionally loved by God. There is a noticeable difference between the moment someone moves from thinking that they are not worthy of God's love and the moment they believe, even in the tiniest way, that they are unconditionally loved by God just as they are right now. I see freedom begin to become a reality for people when this happens.

Opening to God's love allowed me to move through life differently. It continues to help me do so. God's love is unchanging, and it holds true even when human relationships change, end, or disappoint. The unconditional love of God moves with me and holds me steady when my world and environment change. Being loved by

God gives me an unshakable foundation of warmth, hospitality, light, and mercy.

There is a freedom that followed and continues to follow the realization that this gift of love is freely given and I do not have to measure up to the world's standard that deems me worthy to be loved. There is a freedom in knowing that while I am human, sinful, and in need of God, I am still loved.

This is what I so desperately want my children to understand—what I want all of us to understand. An encounter with God's love transforms us. Opening to God's love enables us to love others in ways we never thought we could and in places we never thought we could. Understanding this kind of love internally propels us outward to share the Good News of this promise with others.

LET'S GO TO THE INNER CHAPEL

Noticing God's Ongoing Love and Creation in My Life

Each of us has a unique set of relationships, life experiences, education, and work. Pause and reflect on the ways God continually creates you and has been with you over your whole life so far.

- Look backward over your life and name the key relationships and people in it. What did they teach you about yourself? About love? About others? About God?

- What were key events in your life? What did you learn from them? How did they inform who you are today? How did you experience God loving you through them?

- What are the moments in which your vocation as single, married, or vowed brought you closer to God? Also recall moments in your vocation that moved you away from God.

- What particular struggles or joys have brought you farther from or closer to God (for example, death, life, divorce, marriage, anniversaries, celebrations, transitions, departures, beginnings)?

Embracing the Promises of God

These Scriptures can encourage you as you read them and pray with them.

- Jeremiah 31:3 // "I have loved you with an everlasting love; / therefore I have continued my faithfulness to you."

- Romans 8:38–39 // "For I am convinced that neither death, nor life, nor angels, nor rulers, nor things present, nor things to come, nor powers, nor height, nor depth, nor anything else in all creation, will be able to separate us from the love of God in Christ Jesus our Lord."

- Isaiah 54:10 // "For the mountains may depart / and the hills be removed, / but my steadfast love shall not depart from you, / and my covenant of peace shall not be removed / says the LORD, who has compassion on you."

13

We Are Seen Fully—and Offered Mercy

I've spent much of my adult life seeking to free myself from the voices of other people and to listen more fully to God's voice. In so many ways, I lived like the woman crippled for eighteen years that we read about in Luke's Gospel. As it says, she had a "spirit that had crippled her for eighteen years. She was bent over and was quite unable to stand up straight" (Luke 13:11). While I was not physically bent over by a spirit, listening to other people's voices over God's was weighing me down, keeping me completely incapable of standing erect.

I attempted time and time again to stand up straight on my own, to believe in the gifts and calls of my life, and to not be incapacitated by the weight and tension of trying to please both the world and God. It was not as if I wasn't making steps to say yes to God's call. I had at this point been in ministry more than eighteen years and had done my fair share of retreats, speaking, and spiritual direction. I had published my first book. There were moments when I leaned in and trusted God's call and stood up straight and strong. But then, time and time again, I would listen to other voices instead of God's, and doing so would inhibit any trust I had in God or in my ability to listen to God, and I would find myself bent over once more.

I found myself, yet again, in this spiritual bent-over position about ten months after my first book came out. The voices of doubt were creeping in big-time as I heard both words of affirmation and words that questioned my ability to write and teach on the contemplative life because of my age and gender. You might think I would be used to those voices; they had been around since I began professional ministry at age twenty-four. While I share at length about those who have encouraged me along the way, the voices that I listened to the most at times were the ones that said things directly to me such as, "You have nothing to offer because you are too young" or "You can minister only to people your children's age" or "What can I possibly learn from you, as I am older than you?"

Those voices were not just making their way into my view of ministry but into other areas of my life as well. They made me feel completely unworthy of God's call but also of my ability to believe in God's love and mercy for me. These voices inhibited my growth in God. I was weighed down by their heaviness and negativity. I was frustrated at my tendency to listen to those voices rather than God's voice. I longed to stop the wrestling and to accept God's gift of mercy and live as the woman set free from her infirmity. This was also God's great longing for me. God wanted me to be free and unhindered in my life and ministry. God longs for us to stand erect. Longs to free us. Longs to unbind and heal us.

Maybe you've been there, or maybe you are currently struggling to believe that God's mercy is available to you. Maybe you are in disbelief that you can be set free from brokenness or a long-held hurt. Maybe you feel that there is no way you can be forgiven for what you have done. Most if not all of us struggle at times to believe that God's mercy is available to us.

At that moment, I struggled to believe that there was any other way to live than being bound by the voices that told me I was not good enough to do what God called me to do. I felt that it was a struggle I would fight for the rest of my life.

For months in prayer, as I went to the inner chapel each day, God whispered words to me about the infinite gift of mercy given to us. Certain lines of Scripture seemed to pierce straight to my heart when I sat with them in the silence with God. I came to trust that these were not just passing words to help me feel better but actual, ongoing promises of God that would bear fruit in my life in a transforming kind of way.

Then one morning I settled into my prayer chair, closed my eyes, and entered my inner chapel. As I sat in the silence, acknowledging God who is always with me, I felt led to pray with Luke's passage about the women bent over for eighteen years. I read the passage over and over again. First, I savored the words that caught my heart: "You are set free from your infirmity" (Luke 13:12). Then I began to imagine the scene, allowing it to unfold in my mind and trusting God's gift of imaginative prayer. I saw myself as the crippled woman, bent over not from a physical ailment but from the weight of the battle of choosing between God's voice or the voices around me. It was as if I kept trying to stand, and I would for a bit, until the weight got to be too much, and I would bend under the weight again.

As the scene continued to materialize in my prayer, I glanced up during one of my attempts to stand erect on my own, and when I did, I caught Jesus looking at me. His loving, kind, compassionate eyes so familiar to me at this point on my faith journey noticed me—*and saw me fully*. As our eyes locked, he said to me, "Woman, you are set free from your infirmity." When I heard those words, something in me shifted. It was as if I had known for a very long time that this was possible, but hearing Jesus' words of mercy, his words of freedom that pulsed through my body, caused something to happen. I could feel myself standing up, and I locked eyes with Jesus. His eyes poured love and mercy into me. He looked at me again and said, "Woman, you are set free from your infirmity. Listen to my voice above any others."

I realized then the healing power of Jesus. That day, I was given a strong and healthy "spiritual" back—a new confidence. Power rippled through me that helped my feet find sure, solid footing again. In that moment, I believed in the mercy of God in a bone-deep kind of way. I felt free.

And while I can't honestly say that I've never become bent over since, crippled by the weight of other voices, I can tell you that this moment in prayer freed me in ways that have radically shifted the direction of my life in the years since. I more easily move through and live the calls of my life because I believe more in what God calls me to do and become. The promise of God that touched me that day is this: God sees and understands me completely and responds to me with mercy.

This was not the first time God helped me understand God's mercy, and I know it will not be the last. God continues to draw us deeper in our understanding and our willingness to listen, pay attention, and to be healed and changed. During that time of imaginative prayer, I recognized Jesus and knew his familiar face from spending time with him daily in the inner chapel for more than two decades. My guess is that the woman crippled for eighteen years had some inklings about Jesus before he interacted with her that moment in the synagogue. Nonetheless, Jesus took the first step by noticing her and also calling to her. That's something for us to remember about this gift of mercy: the first step in receiving it is not ours. The offer of mercy is there long before we believe we are worthy to receive it.

Sometimes our own voice gets in the way of our believing in God's promise of infinite mercy. We sometimes believe that our story is already finished and we can't change it. We are left feeling stuck, paralyzed, bound, and helpless. But wherever we are now, God meets us there—and does not leave us there! God is going to do everything—and I mean *everything*—to set us free from what inhibits us, stops us, and leaves us unfree. God protects against and counteracts our human actions and then offers to us new space and life. God offers us mercy.

The Promise of Mercy

The world is full of chaos and darkness—often the results of human choice. If we rely solely on ourselves, even our best efforts, then we set ourselves up for failure and frustration. If we think the limits of hope end with our own solutions, then we will walk a path of darkness, endless restlessness, longing that is never satisfied, and seeking that offers no fulfillment. I know people who live like this; I'm sure you know people like this too. Sometimes I step into the darkness too, feeling lost, alone, unfulfilled, hopeless, isolated. In his book *Mercy: The Essence of the Gospel and the Key to Christian Life*, Cardinal Walter Kasper says, "Where faith in God evaporates, it leaves behind . . . a void. Without God we are completely and hopelessly handed over to worldly fate, chance, and the impulses of history."[21]

But we are not left to worldly fate or change or impulses of history. We are not left alone, because despite our humanness, our flaws, sins, and bad choices, there is a powerful Presence in our lives. This Presence works against human sin and chooses not to leave things to chance but instead chooses to be intimately involved with us. *There is no void because God is with us.*

---

21. Walter Kasper, *Mercy: The Essence of the Gospel and the Key to Christian Life* (Mahwah, NJ: Paulist Press, 2014), 4.

Mercy means God's refusal to leave us where we are. God will not leave us broken, bruised, exhausted, and tired without any hope for new life or new possibilities. God's mercy means always seeking to make all things new.

Jesus promised, "I will not leave you orphaned" (John 14:18). Jesus is with us in all we are facing. Jesus sees what we see; he also entered the world and experienced it as a human. As he entered the world, he brought inextinguishable light.

The Light Entered the Darkness

As mentioned earlier in St. Ignatius's reflection on the Incarnation, he invites us to imagine the Trinity looking down upon the earth and asks us to notice what the Trinity might see. He says the Trinity sees people laughing, crying, dancing. They see and hear the sounds of the world around us, all the noise of creation and humanity: song, machines, celebration, arguments, cries, shouts of joy. We are invited to hear the groanings of all creation.

The Trinity notice both the gift of life in the world and the darkness within it. They hear the groanings of people crying out for mercy and hope. They refuse to leave the world as it is. In a "divine leap of joy," God decides to send the angel to Mary. In an instant, the Incarnation is set into motion, and the long-awaited promise of the Messiah is fulfilled. Jesus is born. Light enters the darkness in the form of an infant, and as the Gospel of John says,

> All things came into being through him, and without him not one thing came into being. What has come into being in him was life, and the life was the light of all people. The light shines in the darkness, and the darkness did not overcome it. (John 1:3–5)

The light of the world grew in wisdom and grace and developed from the tiny infant placed in Mary's arms to a man who was called to spread God's message. Jesus shattered the darkness of the world with the light of his Good News: his message of mercy.

Jesus' Mission of Mercy

To me, one of the most poignant Scripture passages is found in the Gospel of Luke, where Jesus stands in front of the community he grew up in to let people know who he is and to announce his mission. The sequence in Luke's Gospel is as follows: Jesus is baptized, then led into the desert by the Spirit to be tempted for forty days. Jesus returns from the desert strengthened to begin his mission. One sabbath day he goes to the synagogue and stands to read and is handed a scroll where words from what we now call the Old Testament are written. These words he reads capture the Old Testament prophecy of the Messiah coming.

> The Spirit of the Lord is upon me,
>   because he has anointed me
>   to bring good news to the poor.
>
> He has sent me to proclaim release to the captives
>   and recovery of sight to the blind,
>   to let the oppressed go free,
>
> to proclaim the year of the Lord's favor.
>
> —Luke 4:18–19

After reading these words, Jesus rolls up the scroll and then sits down and says, "Today this scripture has been fulfilled in your hearing" (Luke 4:21). Jesus announces his mission of mercy and that he is the one they have all been waiting for. Instead of rejoicing in the Good News being brought to them, his listeners are so angered that they run him out of town.

My heart always hurts a bit for both Jesus and the people that day. The people miss the Good News that is standing right in front of them. They miss Jesus as the face of mercy. Jesus, who knows exactly who he is and knows what he can offer people, is completely misunderstood and rejected. It always makes me wonder, *How many times do we miss the promise of mercy that is offered to us today? How many times is Jesus literally standing right in front of us, fully seeing us, and offering us mercy—and yet we reject the idea that mercy or hope is even possible?*

Isn't what Jesus announced that day the very thing we long for? Aren't we longing for good news in our poverty, whatever that may look like? Aren't we hoping to be released from whatever holds us captive? Aren't we aching to see the truths to which we are blind? Aren't we yearning to be set free from whatever binds us?

Jesus' mission was to the poor, the captive, the blind, the oppressed, the brokenhearted, the mourning. Jesus' promise of mercy is for each of us right now. We are the ones physically and spiritually poor who need a Savior. We are the ones held captive by sin. We are the ones burdened. We are the ones aching with brokenness. We are the ones grieving and mourning. We are the ones in need of mercy. We are the ones seeking to be made well.

But like the people in the synagogue at Nazareth that day who rejected Jesus, we are not always sure if we are ready to accept the promise of mercy given to us. Fortunately, Jesus does not give up on us, fully sees us and our needs, and offers us mercy.

Jesus Sees Us as We Really Are: Give Me a Drink

I can think of no better Scripture to describe Jesus fully seeing us than the Samaritan woman at the well in John's Gospel (John 4:1–42). Jesus sits at the well, tired from his journey. A woman from Samaria comes to the well to draw water, and he says to her, "Give me a drink." This woman does not know that her life is about to change, that she is about to be fully seen and offered the living drink of mercy she longs for.

Jesus breaks social norms: he communicates with a woman who is not a family member, and he communicates with a Samaritan, someone considered a heretic by good, practicing Jews of the day. Jesus and the woman continue talking about the living water that will quench her thirst permanently. Then Jesus, fully seeing all of her life, asks her to go call her husband and come back. She tells him, "I do not have a husband." Jesus, already knowing this, tells her, "You have had five husbands and the one you have now is not your husband" (John 4:18). As their conversation develops, she tells him that she knows the Messiah is coming. Jesus tells her, "I am he." She leaves her water jug at the well and goes into town, telling people, "Come and see a man who told me everything I have done." Because of being fully seen by Jesus and offered mercy through an encounter with him, the woman is transformed, and many others come to believe in Jesus because of this transformation.

The woman at the well reminds me of the lies we tell ourselves about our identity. Lies that I get caught up in telling myself all the time, and I hear others struggling with as well. Henri Nouwen, a priest, professor, and writer, explains that we tell ourselves five lies upon which we base our identity.

1. I am what I have.
2. I am what I do.
3. I am what other people say or think of me.
4. I am nothing more than my worst moment.
5. I am nothing less or more than my best moment.[22]

---

22. Henri Nouwen, *Who Are We?: Henri Nouwen on Our Christian Identity* (Learn25, 2017), Audible audiobook.

The woman at the well reminds me of these lies we tell ourselves about our identity, our worthiness to receive love, and our ability to receive mercy. How often are our identity and worth shaped by what someone tells us we are or by something we've done? I cannot imagine all that the Samaritan woman might have told herself about who she was. As a Samaritan, she was looked down on by the Jews; as a woman, she was told in many ways that she was not as important as a man. Also, she had multiple marriages and divorces. Given the cultural norms of the day, the woman at the well had many voices telling her she was not good enough. Jesus went against everything that the social norms told him about this woman's identity. He engaged her in conversation because he loved her. He saw her for who she was. He offered her mercy. He healed and transformed her.

When Jesus saw me that day in prayer, bent over like the crippled woman, believing lies about my identity and worth, he saw me fully as I was. He saw me as God's child; he also saw me as someone in need of healing. He reminded me who I was, offered me mercy, and healed and transformed me.

Jesus does the same for every one of us. Not just the woman at the well. Not just me. *Every one of us.* Jesus breaks through these lies to our identity, to our worth, and to our belief that mercy is available to us. He seeks to simply offer us mercy by letting us know who we are: a person fully seen and loved by Jesus.

It does not matter what we have: possessions, past experiences, education, or work experiences. It does not matter what we do: for a living, with our life, with our choices. It does not matter what people say about us: whether it is the best compliment or the worst insult. Jesus reminds us that we are *more* to him than the worst thing we've ever done and *even more* than the best moment of our lives. Our identity is wrapped up in the mere fact that we are fully seen just as we are and loved unconditionally anyway.

Just as Jesus engaged with the woman at the well by asking, "Give me a drink," Jesus seeks to engage us. By acting first, as Jesus always does, he drew her into a relationship and helped her see herself exactly as she was and how he loved her and offered her the living water of this relationship. This is what Jesus does to us. He helps us see ourselves through his gentle, loving eyes and calls forth all that inhibits us from seeing our own belovedness in the eyes of God. Jesus sees us the way he saw the woman at the well: the people we are in God.

Jesus Sees Our Need for Healing: Do You Want to Be Made Well?

In John's Gospel, we read the story of a man who has been ill thirty-eight years. Jesus encounters him by a pool known to have healing powers. This sick man has been there for a long time waiting to be able to enter the waters when they are "stirred up" and be healed. Jesus notices him and asks him, "Do you want to be made well?" His response is, "Sir, I have no one to put me in the pool when the water is stirred up; and while I am making my way, someone else steps down ahead of me." Jesus says to him, "Stand up, take your mat and walk" (John 5:1–16).

How often do we feel like the man by the pool, desiring to be made well and yet attempting to get to the healing waters on our own? Sometimes we desire to be made well from physical injury or illness. Other times, the burden we are holding is so heavy that we feel emotionally, mentally, or spiritually sick from carrying it alone. Perhaps it is our grief and mourning that weigh us down, and we wonder if we will ever be well again.

When life weighs us down and we feel consumed by darkness, we can sometimes think that it is our task alone to get to the light, the source of healing. It's not. The man who had been ill for thirty-eight years didn't ever make it into the waters, but he *was* healed by the Person standing right next to him. Jesus noticed him, witnessed his pain, saw the deepest desires of the man's heart, and responded to those desires by healing him.

Far too often, we forget that Jesus is standing right next to us, seeing our pain and understanding our deep desire for mercy. The only step we need to take is to answer the question that Jesus asked the man that day: "Do you want to be made well?" (John 5:6). God does not force us to action, even when that action might bring us healing. God offers mercy, forgiveness, and healing, but do we desire them? Are we willing to receive God's help?

We can rest assured that God is laboring for us to help us get to the healing waters, to help us see the light in the darkness, and to help us know the step forward. We may think that we have to accomplish something or get to a certain point of progress or maturity or understanding in order to "be made well." But God acts on our behalf right now, working with us as we are, not as we think we should be. We simply have to remember that Jesus is already there with us, offering an extended hand in the darkness. God desires us to be made well. What about you? Do you desire to be made well?

What does being made well look like for you right now?

- Do you desire physical healing for yourself or someone else?
- Do you seek to be free from something that binds you?
- Do you need help seeing light in a dark situation?
- Do you desire to be unbound from something that holds you captive?
- Do you need strength to get through a tough situation?
- Are you struggling to forgive yourself or someone else?

We can have confidence that Jesus is standing right here with us. He is in the inner chapel, posing the same question to us as he did to the man who had been ill thirty-eight years. How might we respond to the question Jesus asks: "Do you want to be made well?"

Jesus Sees Our Capacity to Sin: "Woman, Where Are They?"

In John's Gospel, we read of a woman caught in adultery. The law's punishment for this sin was death by stoning. Jesus doesn't speak but simply bends over and begins to write on the ground with his finger. As people continue to question him, he stands and says, "Let anyone among you who is without sin be the first to throw a stone at her." One by one the crowd leaves, and Jesus is left alone with the woman. He asks her, "Woman, where are they? Has no one condemned you?" (John 8:1–10).

As hard as it may be for us to face this, we must name this reality: our capacity to sin. Jesus knew this about the woman and the crowd gathering to stone her. Jesus knows this about each of us. We have this propensity to break down our relationship with God and others, to turn away from God, and to fail to love God, others, and ourselves. Sin causes problems for us personally, communally, and globally.

In the first week of the Spiritual Exercises, we are invited to reflect on our personal experience of sin and comprehend sin not with our heads but with our hearts. We are invited to see sin as God sees it within the context of God's love. Ignatius invites us to take a hard look at our lives and the realities of sin, but not before we have a full understanding of God's unconditional love for us. Before we face our sin, we need to understand that who we are is not rooted in what we have done or not done but in simply being loved by God.

When I lead someone through the Nineteenth Annotation of the Spiritual Exercises, the person spends six weeks praying on God's love before we delve into the material of the "first week," which is on sin and mercy. St. Ignatius is not wanting us to get so overwhelmed with our past choices that our sorrow turns to self-hate or despair. Rather, we remember that God loves us and seeks to free us from anything that blocks our growth in God.

When Desires Become Idols

Sin is a disruption of God's plans for us. Sometimes it happens when we turn away from God, but most often it occurs when we run after false idols, and when we do this, we unravel God's hopes and plans for us. St. Ignatius calls these *disordered attachments*. Disordered attachments can be our desires, our limited hopes, our possessions, our plans, our relationships, or our ambitions. Ultimately, they are people, desires, or things that we become more attached to than we are to God.

Let's think back to the First Principle and Foundation that we mentioned first in chapter 6. These two paragraphs of the First Principle and Foundation illustrate what I mean by disordered attachments.

> All the things in this world are gifts from God, presented to us so that we can know God more easily and make a return of love more readily. As a result, we appreciate and use all these gifts of God insofar as they help us develop as loving persons. But if any of these gifts become the center of our lives, they displace God and so hinder our growth toward our goal.[23]

St. Ignatius invites us to see and notice all the gifts in the world that God gives us. God's gifts can help us develop into loving persons and also help us grow in our relationship with God, if the gifts are used appropriately. What God asks of us is to place God at the center of our lives and let all the gifts revolve around God at the center.

---

23. David L. Fleming, SJ, *Draw Me into Your Friendship: A Literal Translation and a Contemporary Reading of the Spiritual Exercises* (Chestnut Hill, MA: Institute of Jesuit Sources, 1996).

Let's take a closer look at what this means in real life. Each of us is given gifts and innate desires that motivate us to act in life, desires such as

- To be esteemed
- To be successful
- To fear failure
- To please people
- To be financially well off
- To be understood
- To be praised
- To always be right
- To be a person "in the know"
- To be in relationship with others
- To appreciate specific gifts or objects
- To organize
- To care for our health[24]

While any of these desires are good by themselves, where we find ourselves in a heap of trouble is when one or more of these replaces God as the center of life. Instead of living with our end goal in mind, to live with God forever, we end up pursuing a desire. Instead of seeking to please God, we seek the esteem of others. Instead of trying to do what God asks, we seek success in the world. Instead of following Christ, we become focused on trying to avoid failure, to please others, to accumulate wealth, to be in control, to be right, to collect knowledge, and on and on. Perhaps, even, instead of letting God be the center of our lives, we let another relationship become the hub, putting

---

24. Adapted from list in Joseph Langford, M.C., *I Thirst: Forty Days with Mother Teresa* (Denver: Augustine Institute, 2019), 20–21.

all kinds of insane pressure on another person to validate us, to make us feel worthy, or to make us feel lovable.

Let me tell you. It is way too easy to let one of these gifts given to us by God slip into the center of our lives. When we let someone other than God guide our lives or let something (a desire, a tangible item, a gift) become our goal, we are in for, as Boppy would say, "a whole heap of trouble." These people or things become like golden calves that we end up worshipping, even if we never planned to do that.

Our awareness of this capacity to sin leads us right into our need for a Savior. Being aware of our sinfulness is part of accepting our own poverty, that we are utterly dependent on God to overcome our sin and receive mercy. God's mercy frees us, and it also helps us become aware of our sinful tendencies. God gives us sight to see ourselves as God sees us. We learn to see our worth and belovedness but also whatever gets in the way of our receiving God's love and mercy.

Jesus Sees Our Blindness: What Do You Want Me to Do for You?

In Mark's Gospel, we read the story of Jesus encountering a blind man, Bartimaeus, on the road to Jericho. Jesus passes by him, and the man cries out, "Jesus, son of David, have mercy on me!" Jesus calls Bartimaeus to him and asks, "What do you want me to do for you?" Bartimaeus answers, "My teacher, let me see again." Jesus tells him, "Go; your faith has made you well." Bartimaeus regains his sight and follows Jesus (Mark 10:46–52).

Jesus sees our many forms of blindness just as he saw Bartimaeus's physical blindness. Our blindness is often the inability to see what we are putting at the center of our lives instead of God. Jesus sees what inhibits our growth in relationship with him. Jesus calls us to him, the way he called Bartimaeus to him. He asks us, "What do you want me to do for you?" as he sees us struggling and wrestling with sin. He invites us to see our sin so that we can be made well.

God wants us to center our lives around God and to act in a way that leads us further down a path of faith. The Holy Spirit supports us on our faith journey. We are never alone on the path of faith, and God is with us, helping us take steps forward. An important part of our faith journey is learning how God supports us through the work of the Holy Spirit. In essence, the Holy Spirit helps open our eyes to anything that keeps us from staying centered on God.

One of the ways the Holy Spirit helps us is to show us when we have made a choice or a decision that does not lead us closer to God. Often the support of the Holy Spirit comes through a feeling even more than actual sight. We feel the support of the Holy Spirit awakening us to our sinfulness through restlessness that often feels like remorse or the sting of conscience. When our restlessness is due to a choice we have made that is not in alignment with who we are in God, we might notice feelings of

- guilt
- disquiet
- remorse
- regret or
- sorrow

While these feelings are uncomfortable, they can be gifts of the Holy Spirit that help us wake up to something we've done or said that inhibits our growth in God. This type of restlessness might show up when we are seeking to center our life around God but notice some part of life that is still self-focused. God shows us that we are holding too tightly to something or someone. Restlessness might appear when we act in a sinful way and hurt our relationship with God or another person.

When we identify that the source of our restlessness is due to a choice we made, something we said, or a way we acted that makes us feel guilty, remorseful, or sorrowful, our invitation is to act differently. If we sin, we are called to turn from that sin and make a different choice. Or perhaps we said something that we regret. We might find that to calm the restlessness, we need to ask for forgiveness—of ourselves, of God, and maybe of the person we hurt—and say we are sorry.

Even though we are sinful people, God still loves us and offers us forgiveness. God seeks to free us from sinful choices, from deep hurts or wounds, from fears, and from brokenness. God's gift of mercy means that no matter what is going on in our lives, in our world, and in our communities, God is working within us to birth new life and healing.

Our acknowledgment of our sinfulness helps us understand our need for God, the great liberator of our brokenness. God's offer of mercy to each of us frees us so that we can more easily follow Jesus.

Jesus Seeks to Enter Our Brokenness: The Grace of Sorrow

God longs to free us from our own sinfulness. God also longs to enter our hurt, brokenness, and pain—in order to heal us. Some of our pain is due to our own sinful capacity as humans. Sometimes the brokenness we experience is not caused by us or our actions but is simply the result of life's journey and the risk of being in relationships. Sometimes what we feel is the ripple effect of another person's choices. Sometimes our sorrow is the result of our listening to the wrong voices and forgetting who we are.

No matter what we name as our brokenness, God sees it and seeks to enter it and to heal it. God wants to pour the soothing balm of mercy upon what binds us, what has deeply hurt us, and what burdens us. The need for healing might be grief of loss, broken relationship, betrayal, or abandonment. Healing also must occur where our own sinfulness has caused harm.

During the First Week of the Spiritual Exercises of St. Ignatius, the kind of sadness that God allows us to feel when we are being awakened to a sinful tendency or a deep hurt calls forth in us an urge to change. This is the gift of sorrow. Noticing and naming our sorrow can be painful. It can also bring a sense of our helplessness to change anything by ourselves. In essence, it brings to light our dependency on God, our need for God's mercy.

The graces we pray for in the First Week are to feel the deep sorrow and confusion that come from our sinfulness. We even pray for the grace to grieve as God does.

As we see what inhibits our growth in God and we begin to name where we are in need of God's mercy, St. Ignatius invites us to take our sorrow directly to God so we can discern our response. I invite us to go now to our inner chapel and bring to God whatever need we have named, whatever aspect of life needs God's mercy. Go to God, and name where you are seeking the Light to enter your darkness. Know that the very desire for God to enter is God seeing you fully as you are and seeking to offer you the promise of mercy.

LET'S GO TO THE INNER CHAPEL

Triple Colloquy

St. Ignatius offers a beautiful prayer tool called the triple colloquy. *Colloquy* simply means conversation. He invites us to take the sorrow we feel over our brokenness, the sin we have named in ourselves, or the sin we see in the world into our prayer. As we carry the areas of our lives and the world that are in need of God's mercy to prayer, we pause and have three intimate conversations: first with Mary, then with Jesus, and then with God. At the end of each conversation we ask,

What have I done for Christ?
What am I doing for Christ?
What ought I do for Christ?

I invite you to get quiet and go to your inner chapel. As you lean in to God's promise of being fully seen and loved, bring your needs for mercy to Mary, then to Jesus, and then to God. As you talk to each one of them, end your conversation with the three questions St. Ignatius offers us. Listen to their responses to you.

Embracing the Promise of Mercy

These Scriptures can encourage you as you read them and pray with them.

- Mark 3:1–6 // Jesus heals the man with the withered hand.
- Deuteronomy 30:15–20 // "See, I have set before you today life and prosperity, death and adversity."
- Psalm 32 // The joy of forgiveness—"Happy are those whose transgression is forgiven, / whose sin is covered. / Happy are those to whom the LORD imputes no iniquity, / and in whose spirit there is no deceit."
- Mark 5:25–34 // Jesus cures the hemorrhaging woman.

14

We Have a Companion
in Our Suffering

A gift of my grandfather's brain cancer was that he had very little pain. One Thursday morning, I received a call from his sitter. She told me that when my grandfather woke up, the left side of his face was completely swollen and red. It was swollen so much that his ear was hard to see, as if the skin around it had swallowed it. I rushed over to my grandparents' house. I used my special knock on the door as always, but this time my grandmother answered the door with a panicked and frantic look on her face. She opened the door and rushed me into the sunporch, where Boppy's hospice bed was set up. I heard him moaning before I saw him. As I approached the bed, I could see his legs restlessly kicking around as he groaned in pain. I came to the left side of his bed and saw that his face was red and swollen. As he groaned, he kept touching his face over and over again. I leaned in so he could see me, as his eyesight had begun to weaken over recent weeks. He saw and heard it was me, and he said, "Hey, Becksa!" just as he always did. Immediately he followed with, "I love you. I love you, Becksa." I told him, "I love you, Boppy."

For the next several hours, I stayed with him, lifting his legs to help with the restlessness, offering him pain meds, and offering any words of comfort I could. The entire time he was restless and in pain, he kept saying to me, "I love you. I love you, Becksa." Over and over again he told me, and I told him the same. In the moment, the fleeting thought of what this meant passed through my mind, but it wasn't until weeks later that I understood the magnitude of his ability to share his love for me in the middle of the most significant pain of his life. That day was the last day Boppy spoke. Hours after the restlessness and the swelling on his face began, he slipped into a coma. He passed away six days later. The last words he ever said to me were *I love you.*

One night, weeks after Boppy died, I sat listening to the words of Jesus' passion during the Holy Triduum. The scene of Jesus hanging on the cross hit me like never before. In John's Gospel, there is a moment when Jesus is hanging on the cross and Mary, his mother, is there.

> When Jesus saw his mother and the disciple whom he loved standing beside her, he said to his mother, "Woman, here is your son." Then he said to the disciple, "Here is your mother." And from that hour the disciple took her into his own home. (John 19:25–30)

The gesture of love from Jesus in his agony and pain on the cross echoed a similar gesture of love I experienced weeks earlier from my grandfather. Both in their final moments, aching with pain, they offered words of love. My grandfather reminded me of his love for me. Jesus ensured that his mother and friend were taken care of and not alone. Both somehow, while in their suffering, companioned others who suffered.

When I came home from Mass, I read Luke's version of the Passion and found another moment when Jesus, while dying on the cross, showed enduring love to those around him.

> One of the criminals who were hanged there kept deriding him and saying, "Are you not the Messiah? Save yourself and us!" But the other rebuked him, saying, "Do you not fear God, since you are under the same sentence of condemnation? And we indeed have been condemned justly, for we are getting what we deserve for our deeds, but this man has done nothing wrong." Then he said, "Jesus, remember me when you come into your kingdom." He replied, "Truly I tell you, today you will be with me in Paradise." (Luke 23:39–43)

This is the foundation of everything in regard to our faith: the depth in which God loves us. The lengths to which God will go to show us this love by becoming a companion to us when we suffer. The same way God companioned Jesus in his suffering, God companions us in ours. We are never alone in what we are facing because Jesus who suffered walks with us.

Fix Our Eyes on Jesus

We all encounter suffering, either our own or someone else's. Perhaps our suffering or the suffering we witness is not like Jesus' agony on the cross or like my grandfather's cancer journey, but in our own way we experience and witness hurt, abandonment, betrayal, loss, doubt, fear, or pain. It is hard to endure suffering and also watch another person suffer. If it is our own suffering we are facing, we tend to yearn for someone to stay with us, be present to us, and listen to us. If we are faced with another's suffering, we may be invited to stay with the other person, to be present, even when no words can be offered. No matter which role we play, we can rest assured that Jesus is our companion in it. Jesus who was entirely human experienced the full range of humanity, good and bad.

Toward the end of my grandfather's sickness I confided in Sr. Beth, a Carmelite sister I know, that I was afraid to accompany my grandfather to his death. She took my hand and looked at me with the kindest eyes and spoke to me with great gentleness: "Yes, you can . . . you have walked with Jesus, your friend, to his death when you made the Spiritual Exercises, and you walk with him each year during Lent."

She asked, "What is the invitation as you accompany Jesus to his death?" I wasn't able to think clearly, so she continued: "You fix your eyes on Jesus. He will not only teach you about how to go through suffering but he will also remind you that he understands what you face and knows how to accompany others in their suffering." Her words of wisdom: to simply keep my eyes fixed on Jesus and stay with my grandfather. Walk with Boppy by leaning on Jesus, who walked with both of us.

Her wisdom reminded me so much of the wisdom of the third week of the Spiritual Exercises, where we are invited to simply be with Jesus in his suffering. During the third week of the Spiritual Exercises, St. Ignatius suggests that I ask for the grace to be with Jesus in his sufferings and to understand that Jesus suffered for me. Walking this closely with Jesus as he faces the last moments of his life—from the Last Supper through his passion and death—illuminates the depth of suffering he went through. Think about all that one man experienced:

- saying yes to a relationship with God that gave him identity, purpose, and clarity of his call

- being misunderstood by family members, friends, and community because of his call

- gathering his close friends around him and inviting them into an intimate friendship with him, only to be abandoned, denied, and betrayed by them

- standing up for those who were considered outcasts—the lepers, prostitutes, sinners, tax collectors, physically sick—and in doing so becoming as marginalized as they were

- healing and curing the disabled and paralyzed, and receiving in his own body lashes, thorns, and the cross, which broke his body so that he needed the very healing he offered others

- comforting those who were mourning over lost loved ones, then having to watch his own mother and loved ones witness his suffering, comforting them while in his own pain

When it comes to praying with Jesus' passion, all we are asked to do is *be with Jesus*. Keep our eyes locked and fixed on Jesus. To stay by his side, walking with him, offering whatever comfort we can, the way Veronica wiped his face, the way Simon carried his cross, the way Joseph of Arimathea offered space to bury his dead body.

What I have found by praying the Passion and walking with Jesus through it is how closely the suffering of my own life relates to Jesus' suffering. How, while at times I feel I am alone and the only one holding this suffering, there is someone who gets it. Someone who understands. Someone I am invited to turn to and who wants to be with me in my suffering.

When I walk someone through the third week of the Spiritual Exercises, I witness Jesus' passion becoming a lived reality of the other person's life. Some piece of Jesus' experience connects with their lives. The person's wounds touch Jesus' wounds. Our tender, broken hearts are met with the compassionate love of a friend who understands what we are facing. In prayerful reflection and meditation, Jesus' passion becomes a shared experience of pain, just as a person who lived or is living a similar experience of suffering can compassionately connect with a person in ways others cannot. People can connect through a common experience of pain. Maybe it's two hearts who understand what it is like to watch a loved one fight an addiction or some other health battle. Maybe it's two warriors connecting over the survival of cancer or two people connecting in the courage to rebuild after a natural disaster. Maybe it is the understanding from another who has miscarried or struggled with infertility.

All of us have clubs we wish we didn't belong to—clubs we inadvertently joined through our suffering and pain. What might yours be? Where have you experienced suffering or witnessed another's suffering? Pause for a moment and ask, *Where might Jesus' suffering mirror what this person is going through, or what I am going through?* How might Jesus be able to meet you in this with a compassionate and understanding heart? Do you feel misunderstood as he was? Betrayed or abandoned? Do you wrestle with physical pain? Maybe you face the task of forgiving someone who has deeply hurt you, as Jesus faced forgiving Peter. Maybe you feel in exile or outcast in some way, simply because of who you are.

How often do we long for our pain to be understood? How often do we seek to be able to articulate to someone else what we're going through? One of life's greatest agonies is the untold story. I've certainly been there, enduring seasons of suffering while desperately longing for someone to understand what I was going through and feeling at a complete loss for words to explain this to someone who had not faced what I was facing.

I remember feeling like this one day as I entered my peer supervision group right around news of new tumor growth, and we were in the agony of not knowing the next steps for my grandfather. I entered that meeting with heaviness in my heart. The opening prayer someone prepared included a reflection question about how we were experiencing Jesus' passion in our lives. When my time came to share, I said, "How come there are no stories in the Bible about someone facing their death? Of someone accompanying another to their death?" The room went quiet and the others looked at me lovingly. One person gently named the obvious for me: *Becky, Jesus did know he was facing his death. So did his mother, Mary. Didn't Jesus walk to his death? Didn't Mary accompany her son to his final breath?* I sat there stunned. I was so wrapped up in the heaviness, sadness, and agony of the unknown that I completely forgot to turn to the ones I love who understood both these things. In that moment, Jesus' passion connected to what my grandfather was facing, and Mary's journey connected to mine.

Instead of barreling through the next few weeks on my own, facing the unknown while we waited to find out if Grandfather had more options for treatment, I turned to my companion, my friend: Jesus, the one who understood what it was like to beg for something to pass. Deep calls to deep. The depth of longing for my loved one connected deeply with the longing of Mary's heart for her son. I saw and understood Jesus meeting Boppy in his suffering in a way I never had before.

It is hard to articulate the strength that this realization gave me in that moment and in the many months ahead. I understood, in a whole new way, this promise of God for me and for Boppy, but also for all of us. We have a companion in our suffering. A confidant. A friend. A compassionate, listening heart meeting us in our spiritual poverty and every other kind of poverty we might face. This gift of companionship in my spiritual poverty gave me strength.

Spiritual Poverty

Encountering the suffering of my grandfather brought me to a place of spiritual poverty. To me, spiritual poverty is utter reliance on God. We encounter spiritual poverty in those moments when no amount of money or power or influence or medicine or anything else can change the reality of the circumstances. I think we feel invincible at times as human beings, thinking that we can control all situations due to our intelligence, finances, relationships, or power.

From my experience and from listening to others describe their experiences, I believe that at some point every person is stripped of everything and faced with the truth that we utterly depend on God. I reached this point when the doctor let us know that we had come to a moment where treatments would hurt my grandfather far more than they would help him. At such a moment, utter despair hits because you know that you are out of options. I remember trembling inside as I scooted my chair up next to Boppy's hospital bed to deliver the news to him and to let him know he had a choice to make. I feared seeing his reaction, and I feared that I would lose my composure when I explained there were no more treatment options, when I asked, *Do you want to enter hospice at home or at a hospice center?* I watched Boppy hit this moment when, after years of working hard, pulling himself out of childhood poverty, saving money, and living a comfortable life, he realized that there was nothing he could do to change the outcome.

In such moments, when we are helpless to change our situation, we encounter spiritual poverty. We understand then, in a tangible way, how desperately we need a Messiah. How urgently we yearn for someone who will bring hope and light into a dark situation. Have you experienced such a moment or watched someone else hit this point?

Spiritual poverty strips you down to your bones, making you feel raw and vulnerable and weak. And yet, it is here in our utter human weakness that we become strong—not through brute human force or through our personal gumption to push through. We become strong through leaning fully on the promise that we are not alone in our suffering.

It reminds me of the lines of Scripture in the letter from Paul to the Philippians:

> I know what it is to have little, and I know what it is to have plenty. In any and all circumstances I have learned the secret of being well-fed and of going hungry, of having plenty and of being in need. I can do all things through him who strengthens me. (Philippians 4:12–13)

Paul writes honestly about life as we all experience it. We have moments of abundance, joy, and calm. We also have moments when we feel the depth of our need for someone to help us. We encounter our dependence on God and on others. Paul's life experience taught him that his strength in moments of both abundance and suffering came from Jesus. Paul learned that God's grace is enough. Often it is not until we are on the other side of the dark situation, when light gives clarity to what we have experienced, that we realize that the grace God gave us was more than enough. Kevin O'Brien, SJ, says that suffering empties us so that God can fill us with life and love.[25] As I reflect on suffering in my own life, I understand this to be true. Suffering brings us face-to-face with our dependence on God, and as we meet our own weakness and need, we are met also with the grace that comes from the strength of God's companionship in our suffering.

In one of my grandfather's early ICU stays after a tumor was removed, the hospital chaplain gave us a prayer by St. Francis de Sales. Sometimes the great writers and saints who went before us give us words that capture our hearts' deepest desires and prayers. They give us words that help us cling to the promises of God when we cannot voice the words we long to pray. This is how I felt when the chaplain

---

25. Kevin O'Brien, SJ, *The Ignatian Adventure: Experiencing the Spiritual Exercises of Saint Ignatius in Daily Life* (Chicago: Loyola Press, 2011), 159.

put this prayer into my hands. It became the prayer that I turned to many times to help me pray when I no longer could speak the words on my own. It gave me strength and hope. It helped me get through the moments when I felt I could not go on.

I offer it here now for you. May it bring you the deep comfort it brought me and continues to bring me. May it help you trust the promise of God's companionship in whatever you are facing right now.

> Do not look forward in fear to the changes of life;
> rather look to them with full hope that as they arise,
>   God, whose very own you are, will lead you safely
>   through all things;
> And when you cannot stand it, God will carry you
>   in His arms.
> Do not fear what may happen tomorrow;
> The same everlasting Father who cares for you today
>   will take care of you today and every day.
> He will either shield you from suffering or will give you
>   unfailing strength to bear it.
> Be at peace and put aside all anxious thoughts and
>   imaginations.[26]
>
> —St. Francis de Sales

I can tell you this—I know that while I would not choose suffering, those moments transformed me profoundly because of the grace and love God poured into my life at that time. It is the grace of God pouring into me over the course of my whole life and especially during the eighteen months of walking with my grandfather that gives me the courage and the ability to write these words.

---

26. *Selected Letters of St. Francis de Sales*, trans. Elisabeth Stopp, Letter #106.

Suffering Makes Us Compassionate

This promise of a companion in our suffering does not end with the darkness of Good Friday and Jesus' death. This promise of companionship continues even if our lives linger in Holy Saturday for a long time when we find ourselves stuck between our loss and the hope of new life.

New life does come. One sign of new life that comes after suffering is that we become more loving, more faithful, more generous, and more compassionate. St. Ignatius says, "There are truths that can be discovered only through suffering or from the critical vantage point of extreme situations."[27] I can honestly say that there are truths I learned through suffering that—while I do not want to go through such pain again—I consider great gifts of understanding, for which I am grateful.

The biggest grace given to me is the grace of compassion. I see suffering making some people hard and bitter, but I believe that suffering can create a compassionate heart when we allow the experience to turn us to God. Jesus suffered, and out of this his compassionate love for each of us is poured into us as a source of hope, strength, and companionship. The suffering we experience becomes transformed into wells of compassion for us to share as we are invited to companion others in their suffering.

As Pope Francis reminds us in *On Hope*, "God the Father comforts by raising comforters."[28] How might God be inviting each of us to use our suffering to now become a source of comfort and compassion for others?

---

27. Kevin O'Brien, SJ, *The Ignatian Adventure: Experiencing the Spiritual Exercises of St. Ignatius in Daily Life* (Chicago: Loyola Press, 2011), 218.
28. Pope Francis, *On Hope* (Chicago: Loyola Press, 2017), 3.

The promise of Jesus companioning us in our suffering gives us strength to stay with others in theirs. I am not sure I could have stayed with Boppy and walked with him had I not known and trusted the power of Jesus' companionship to both of us.

Let's turn now to some practical tools we use to go to our inner chapel to deepen our understanding of the promise of God's companionship.

LET'S GO TO THE INNER CHAPEL

Colloquy with Christ Crucified

St. Ignatius invites us to have a conversation, or colloquy, with Jesus on the cross as we pray with his passion or with our own "passion moments." Remember that Jesus understands and relates to our experiences.

I invite you to reflect on where your life is connecting with Jesus' passion. Or where has it connected to Jesus' passion?

- Are you having an agony-in-the-garden moment? Begging for something to pass?
- Do you feel betrayal by a friend or a loved one as Jesus experienced with Peter and Judas?
- Do you find yourself struggling to forgive, the way Jesus was asked to do on the cross?
- Do you feel abandoned, the way Jesus was by his friends and followers?
- Are you experiencing any kind of exile, the way Jesus was exiled from his community?
- Do you feel you are being cast out the way Jesus was?
- Are you an immigrant or refugee, seeking refuge in ways Jesus did as he longed to belong somewhere among a divided people?
- Are you enduring physical pain?
- Are you watching another loved one suffer, as Mary watched her son?

Once you reflect on where your life and Jesus' life connect, go to your inner chapel. Turn to a conversation with Jesus on the cross. Talk to him openly and honestly about whatever is stirring in your heart.

Here are St. Ignatius's words to guide your prayer.

Imagine Christ our Lord present before you on the cross, and begin to speak with him, asking how it is that though He is the Creator, He has stooped to become man, and to pass from eternal life to death here in time, that thus He might die for our sins.

I shall also reflect upon myself and ask:

What have I done for Christ?
What am I doing for Christ?
What ought I do for Christ?

As I behold Christ in his plight, nailed to the cross, I shall ponder upon what presents itself to my mind. (SE #53)[29]

Close with an Our Father.

Embracing the Promise of Companionship in Our Suffering

These Scriptures can encourage you as you read them and pray with them.

- Isaiah 43 // "When you pass through the waters, I will be with you; / and through the rivers, they shall not overwhelm you."
- Psalm 23 // "Even though I walk through the darkest valley, / I fear no evil; / for you are with me."
- Revelation 21:1–7 // "God himself will be with them; / he will wipe every tear from their eyes. / Death will be no more; / mourning and crying and pain will be no more."

Prayers for Support

I've come to think that the only, the supreme, prayer
we can offer up, during these hours
when the road before us is shrouded in darkness,
is that of our master on the cross:
"In manus tuas commendo spiritum meum."
[Into your hands I commend my spirit.]
To the hands that broke and gave life to the bread,
that blessed and caressed, that were pierced; . . .
to the kindly and mighty hands that reach down
to the very marrow of the soul—that mould and create—
to the hands through which so great a love is transmitted—
it is to these that it is good to surrender our soul,
and above all when we suffer or are afraid.
And in so doing there is a great happiness and a great merit.[30]
                                        —Pierre Teilhard de Chardin, SJ

Let nothing disturb you, nothing frighten you, all things are passing, God is unchanging. Patience gains all; nothing is lacking to those who have God: God alone is sufficient.

—Teresa of Ávila

---

29. Louis J. Puhl, *The Spiritual Exercises of St. Ignatius* (Chicago, IL: Loyola Unviversity Press, 1951), 28.

30. Michael Harter, SJ, ed., *Hearts on Fire: Praying with Jesuits* (Chicago: Loyola Press, 1993, 2004), 132.

15

Each of Us Has a Unique Call

I cannot teach area and perimeter for the rest of my life. These words pounded in my head while twenty-four sixth graders stared at my back as I drew the next geometric figure for them to solve. I swallowed hard to fight back tears before I turned to face them again. I tried to stuff what was becoming crystal clear both in my prayer and in my daily life: teaching was not for me.

When I admitted this to myself, I felt like a failure. I had earned an undergraduate and a graduate degree in education. Both my mom and my grandmother were teachers, and my plan was to follow in their footsteps. The reality was, even back in college when I was choosing a major, I'd had an inkling that I was not on the right path. People would ask me what I wanted to do, and I often talked about doing something in ministry. Attending a public university, I had no clear path to major in a degree that would support me on this journey, so I picked education instead.

Now I can look back on the classes I took and the student teaching I did and get a pretty clear idea that this was not what I was built for. The classes and teaching drained me tremendously. I enjoyed aspects of what I learned in my education training, such as human development, psychology, and learning styles. But I always felt a bit out of place watching the energy of others in my classes as they applied these topics to teaching children. It was as if I knew even then that all that I learned would be applied later to something else. What I noticed that day as I wrote on the board was a growing depth of tiredness every day as I continued on a path that I knew deep down was not the one God was calling me to.

What I noticed that day in the classroom mirrored what was beginning to arise in prayer as I spent regular time in my inner chapel. As my involvement in volunteer youth and young-adult ministry around the Diocese of Baton Rouge increased, I felt joy, lightness, and energy. When I would get quiet and meet God in my inner chapel to talk about all this, my heart and mind would often turn to the possibility of full-time ministry. If I gave myself permission to dream of this idea, I would feel hope, joy, peace, and energy.

For over a year I attempted to push this thought to the far recesses of my mind, but God would not let me continue that pattern. And so, in the middle of one of my math classes, clarity hit like a ton of bricks. It was overwhelming and confusing and energizing and scary. It was the middle of the school year; I had not only half the year ahead of me but also no idea what my next steps should be. Maybe you have felt like this when you had clarity that what you were doing was not right for you but you were not sure what to do next, and how.

So, what did I do? I visited my inner chapel frequently. I prayed. I kept asking God, "What is the next right step?" Clarity slowly came. First, with God's affirmation that teaching was not the right fit for me. Second, in helping me work through my feelings of failure as a teacher and of letting people down. Third, in opening up an opportunity that I could say yes to that seemed like a good fit and also helped our family make ends meet financially.

I would love to say that the opportunity that came was the one that brought me into the world of ministry as a profession, but it was an opportunity to teach and sell Dale Carnegie Courses. During our first year of marriage, my grandfather had gifted Chris and me with an opportunity to take this course for a chance to grow and develop our speaking and personal relationship skills. After completing the course, Chris and I were involved as teaching assistants in the courses. After much prayer and discernment, I said yes to the Dale Carnegie opportunity and let my principal know I would not be returning the next school year. Prayer anchored me as I finished out the school year and readied myself for the new job.

A few weeks after the school year ended, I began this new job with a new committed energy, determined to make this one work. I laugh at myself as I write this because the desire to be in ministry was so apparent at this point in my life that I have no idea why I thought this career decision was a good one for me. It didn't take long at all for me to realize the big ole mistake I had made. The desire to work in ministry was so strong that I was doomed to fail at this job. That's pretty much what I did. My boundless energy at the beginning plummeted within weeks of starting, and then I was left with complete despair as I realized the mistake I'd made and how I had chosen not to follow a clear desire from God. I had no idea what to do.

Well, as God's mercy works, my way out of this disastrous mistake came during a hurricane in the fall. Chris and I were hunkering down during the storm when a friend of mine named Charles called me out of the blue. Charles and I knew each other through the youth ministry I volunteered for. He said, "Becky, I want you to come work for me." My heart skipped a beat when he said this because he worked in the Christian Formation Office at the Diocese of Baton Rouge. Even with the clarity of my call, my response to him was, "Charles, I would love to, but I can't. I just started this other job, and I cannot leave it already." He listened to me a bit more and then described what my role would be working for him, reiterating how he felt I would be a good fit for this role, and ended our conversation with an "at least come have lunch with me to discuss it more."

I hung up, stunned, and told Chris what had happened. Where in the world did this invitation come from? Both of us, practical beings that we are, shrugged this off as an impossible opportunity because I had just started a new job. Again, I tried to push the energy and increase in faith and hope back in the crevices of my mind, but God would not leave me alone. The desire just kept growing, as if the Holy Spirit were screaming at me, *HELLLO!!!! When are you going to pay attention to me?*

After a few weeks of feeling very restless and unable to ignore my growing dis-ease, I called Charles and we met for lunch. Needless to say, the rest is history. About a month after that lunch, I received an official offer to work at the diocese, and I began a month after that. Within weeks of starting work at the diocese, I knew I was home and where I was supposed to be. My days were spent offering retreats to youth in the schools and parishes, supporting Directors of Religious Education in our diocese, and doing a slew of other special projects that were all ministry related. During my time at the diocese, I began Young Adult Ministry because I was one of two diocesan employees under the age of forty.

This was a defining moment for me—a moment when God placed a desire in my heart and gave me the gifts, means, and opportunities to act on this desire, and it changed everything. I continued to pray my way through this discernment and check the fruits of the decision. When I look back on that discernment now, I chuckle at how much I fought it. Thank goodness, God kept working on me in prayer and letting me know, through my disquiet and unrest, that I was not on the right path.

This moment helped me get to where I am today, writing this book. This opened the door for me to work with Charis Ministries to bring Ignatian retreats to Baton Rouge for those in their twenties and thirties, and only deepened my love for Ignatian spirituality. I continued to work with Charis Retreats when we moved to Athens, Georgia, and in 2009 began working for Charis Ministries. While in Georgia, I made the Spiritual Exercises, and my retreat work grew to include adults of all ages. Years later, I am still involved in Ignatian retreat ministry.

I don't know why I am surprised about this call to retreat ministry. My friend Stephanie, with whom I cofacilitate Ignatian retreats, often says to me in a completely sarcastic way when I am doubting this call to retreat ministry and wanting to give up, "I want to see you try to stop doing retreat work. Good luck with that! Let me know how that goes for you." As only a dear friend can remind you with such honesty, Stephanie reminds me of the lived promise of God in my life: I have a unique call. She knows that if I were to stop answering this call, I would be very restless and it would snowball into all kinds of searching for meaning.

The call to accompany people on retreats is a thread of my life that I can trace back all the way to when I was seventeen years old as a student minister at my high school, offering retreats for junior high students. When I entered college, I began a retreat team of college students who gave retreats for junior high and high school students. When I entered young adulthood, God called me to offer retreats for my peers and later expanded that call to reach men and women of all ages. Out of that retreat ministry, my call for spiritual direction came and my desire to write grew. Here I am, all these years later, accompanying people through spiritual direction, retreats, and writing. Part of the reason I am writing a second book is to share more about the spirituality, the promises, and the tools that helped me understand my call.

I'm grateful that God never gave up on my coming to understand what my callings are. God won't give up on you either. That's the way God works—not resting until we say yes to the call God has for each one of us. God does not give up on us understanding our gifts and how God is inviting us to use them.

Over the course of my life, jobs, and careers, my gifts and talents have not really changed, nor was the education I received or the experience of my other jobs a waste. The skills I learned in my education classes in college and graduate school are ones I draw on daily: skills such as making a "lesson plan," which in my work involves making a retreat schedule, breaking down topics and themes in bite-size ways for people to understand, or creating handouts to support what I am teaching or talking about. All my study of human development and psychology serves me well in meeting people where they are in ministry and understanding how our physical, mental, and social lives impact who we are. Even my six-month stint at Dale Carnegie continues to support the work I do in regard to building relationships and teaching adults.

What did change was offering my gifts and talents to the service of God. When I began doing that, that's what set me on the path of discovering my call. A wise colleague and fellow spiritual director, Melinda LeBlanc, says, "Our gifts and talents do not change. Sometimes we are not aware of the gifts we have, and God calls them out of us. God calls our gifts out of us for God's use. Our work is to point our gifts to God and offer them to serve God."

Our work of discernment is so often about all the choices and good we can do to respond to God's love for us. What are the choices that will deepen God's life in me? We are always discerning what is the "better way" or the "greater" way to respond to and share what we have generously been given. This brings us to the last part of Fleming's First Principle and Foundation: "Our only desire and our one choice should be this: I want and I choose what better leads to the deepening of God's life in me."[31]

Understanding our call is discovering our deep desires that enable us to be in greater service to God and therefore deepen God within each of us. In Ignatian terms, we are discerning our *magis*, the "more" we are called to in life. How is God inviting me to a more meaningful and joyful life?

But how do we know our gifts and discover the promise that we each have a unique call? St. Ignatius has a lot to say about that, and we are going to unpack it a bit in this chapter.

Ongoing Creation

Something that continues to amaze me about a relationship with Jesus is how he *continues* to call us personally. As mentioned earlier, the call begins with Jesus pointing to the waters of faith, inviting us to walk with him and be in a relationship with him. Jesus doesn't call us one time and then abandon us. He walks with us and guides us into deeper waters of faith. What's exciting is that this invitation is not only about a personal friendship with Jesus but also about inviting us to embrace our call to discipleship in new ways. With each step further into the ocean of faith, ongoing creation is happening.

Recently we took a family road trip out West to visit many of our country's national parks. I stood in awe of God's creative work in places such as the Grand Canyon, Antelope Canyon, and the Red Rocks of Arizona. What struck me about these massive works of God's creation is how they are ever changing, being created moment

---

31. David L. Fleming, SJ, *Draw Me into Your Friendship: A Literal Translation and a Contemporary Reading of the Spiritual Exercises* (Boston: Institute of Jesuit Sources, 1996), 27.

by moment by nature's artistic instruments of wind, water, and fire. What we see of these grand sceneries in nature today will not be the same tomorrow. They are examples of God's ongoing creation in our lives, using the changing elements around them to continue to carve and mold them into what they are today.

God creates us moment by moment too. We are not stagnant, frozen-in-time beings. We are malleable, ongoing works of God's creation. While God's instruments of creation in nature are wind, fire, and water, God uses our gifts, our circumstances, our prayer lives, and our experiences to continue creating us, moment after moment.

God labors on our behalf long before we realize it. God was part of our conception and birth, making us the unique human beings we are—down to our sex, race, hair color, eye color, and personality traits. We had no control over the family we were born into and the city where we were born. God continues creating us moment by moment.

Want to notice God at work in your life and creating you moment by moment? I invite you to look backward over your life and name the key people in it. What did they teach you about yourself? About love? About God?

What about key events in your life? How did events of your past inform who you are now? What you know about God's love for you? What you know about yourself? Your gifts? Your personality traits?

If we look at our life's history, we can notice God's saving hand at work in it. The stories of our lives reveal to us God's ongoing work in us. I have invited you several times throughout the book to look back at your life and acknowledge all the ways God was part of it and part of making you who you are today. In chapter 3, I invited you to create a spiritual autobiography remembering your relationship with God. In chapter 4, I invited you to look at how you learned how to pray. In chapter 9, I invited you to do Hagar's questions, looking back at where you have been in order to understand where you are going. In chapters 11 and 12, I invited you to look at the ways God created you, formed you, and loved you. Now we look back at another aspect of our ongoing creation with God: reviewing our life to see our gifts and callings.

What we find in looking back is that throughout the ongoing creation, there are common threads that tie our unique callings to the work of spreading the Good News. There is not another human being on this planet who looks the same as you do or I do or who has the same experiences and relationships.

As we notice and name God's gift of ongoing creation, we can offer to God all our gifts, experiences, and understandings. The Ignatian prayer that helps us do that is the *Suscipe*, or "Take, Lord" prayer.

Take, Lord, and receive all my liberty,
my memory, my understanding,
and my entire will,
All I have and call my own.
You have given all to me.
To you, Lord, I return it.

Everything is yours; do with it what you will.
Give me only your love and your grace,
that is enough for me.

Our Unique Call to Discipleship

As we are called to be one of Jesus' disciples, we are called to give Jesus our yes to relationship first, and as we do this, we understand what our unique call to discipleship looks like. Think of the first disciples Jesus called. All said yes to following Jesus. Each disciple became a distinctive expression of discipleship, based on that person's gifts. We see Peter's call to discipleship being expressed in his gift of leadership. Thomas's is in asking questions that invoke expressions of faith such as "My Lord and my God!" John's as the steady companion to Jesus standing at the foot of the cross with Jesus' mother to the end. Each says yes to following Jesus and allows his gifts to guide the calling.

If we think beyond the first disciples, we see hundreds of witnesses in our saints who said yes to following Jesus. Each saint, though, was called to a unique response to his or her relationship with Jesus through an expression of service. St. Mother Teresa began her journey of faith at a young age. As Jesus continued to create her moment by moment, she found her unique call to be serving people on the streets of Calcutta and her heart's passion to be quenching Jesus' thirst through caring for his people. Or take St. Ignatius, whose conversion happened later in life, but after laying his sword at the feet of the Black Madonna, he began to understand that his unique call in response to the love he received from God was to education and retreat work, helping people grow in their relationship with God through mind and heart. St. Teresa of Ávila had a passion for helping people learn the art of contemplative prayer. St. Francis of Assisi's yes to God led him to a ministry of hospitality, preaching, and care for creation. Our list would go on and on as we looked at each saint's yes to God and then that person's ongoing expression of discipleship.

But what about today? What about us? So often we think that these calls are set aside for special people like our saints and not for each of us in our ordinary lives. This could not be further from the truth. The saints serve as our great cloud of witnesses, giving us examples of how to live courageous and bold lives of faith. They are not to be examples of holiness that make us feel that we cannot obtain what they did. Each of us has the promise of being personally invited by Jesus into a relationship and being uniquely chosen and called into service to God according to our gifts. Pope Francis writes in his apostolic exhortation *Gaudete et Exsultate*,

There are some testimonies that may prove helpful and inspiring, but that we are not meant to copy, for that could even lead us astray from the one specific path that the Lord has in mind for us. The important thing is that each believer discern his or her own path, that they bring out the very best of themselves, the most personal gifts that God has placed in their hearts, rather than hopelessly trying to imitate something not meant for them.[32]

How often do we try to imitate someone else's call instead of noticing the personal gifts in our own life that God has given us to discern our unique path and call? I'm certainly guilty of this. I look to the saints sometimes and think, *I can never have faith like theirs* or *I can never find my purpose and gifts as they did.* If I'm really honest, there are moments I look at women and men alive today and judge and compare my faith to theirs—feeling at times that they are somehow answering God's call better than I am. It can leave me feeling unworthy, inadequate, and that I am not serving God well.

That's a load of malarkey! You and I have a unique purpose and call. We have a unique expression of what our relationship with Jesus looks like in prayer. Each of us has a specific expression of what service to God looks like. Here are words that I savor over and over again about the small-*s* saints (you and me) since they were published by Pope Francis in *Gaudete et Exsultate*: "Each saint is a mission, planned by the Father to reflect and embody, at a specific moment in history, a certain aspect of the Gospel." Holy wow! Read that one a few times! Each of us is created in such a way that we are being invited to reflect a certain part of the Good News at a specific moment in history. Look around you: think of people you know who are sharing the Good News in all kinds of ways. If you are like me, you might notice the

---

32. Pope Francis, *Gaudete et Exsultate*, 11.

breadth of service and sharing of gifts. Here are a few examples of people I know who demonstrate this to me.

- The parents raising their children
- The man who has a heart for helping women as they leave prison and return to life "beyond the bars," as he calls it
- The teachers I know in schools and parishes who are not only educating young minds but also forming young people in faith
- The friend who sits with and accompanies those in hospice facing their death; the women and men caring for their aging parents
- The couples in relationships
- The women and men getting up every day and heading to work to share their gifts with the world in whatever profession they are called to be in

If we pay attention, we will notice how frequently we encounter people who are expressing aspects of the gospel at a specific moment in history. Pope Francis invites us in *Gaudete et Exsultate* to see the entirety of our life as mission.[33] His blessing to us is "May you come to realize what the word is, the message of Jesus that God wants to speak to the world by your life."[34]

Your unique call is the word that Jesus invites you to speak to the world by your life and calling. It plays out in every relationship you are in, every encounter you have, how you use your gifts, and what you do with your time. The same is true for every other person. This is how we are Jesus' co-laborers in the vineyard. This is how we are his cocreators in building the kingdom of God.

---

33. Pope Francis, *Gaudete et Exsultate*, 23.
34. Pope Francis, *Gaudete et Exsultate*, 24.

I remember one time when I was discerning a call, a spiritual director gently reminded me not to get so caught up in the large mission of life that I miss the mission that is daily and right in front of me. She said, "Remember, you are the only one who can be Brady's mom, Abby's mom, and Mary's mom. You are the only one who is Chris's wife." Those words remind me of St. Mother Teresa's wisdom when people asked her how to do what she did: "Go find your own Calcutta and start by loving those right around you!" So, a piece of my call is to love the spouse I am married to, to love the three children God gave us, and to love the friends and other family members in my life.

And, like anyone reading this book, I have other gifts God invites me to put into the kingdom's service. Although I was called to be Chris's wife and the mom of our children, over the years I discovered my gifts and call to accompany people on retreats, in spiritual direction, and through writing. Those are the calls people can see more easily. Yet I am invited each moment to notice what aspect of the gospel I am being asked to embody. Perhaps, in a broken relationship it is to embody mercy or forgiveness or to a sick loved one to embody compassion and presence or to a discouraged person encouragement and hope.

Each of us has hundreds of opportunities a day to embody a certain aspect of the gospel in a specific moment in history. I invite you to notice and pay attention throughout your day to the many times Jesus gives you to express your faith through the works of your life.

How Do We Know Our Unique Call?

As we learn that Jesus calls us personally, we may wonder how we come to know that call. We come to understand this through discernment. St. Ignatius left our Christian faith the gift of discernment wisdom. While there are entire books that break down his rules of discernment, I would like to give you a few simple overviews that can help you begin.

Discernment begins with understanding the promises. It begins with knowing that God loves us. Discernment is about God's love for us and our response to God's love for us. When we are seeking to discern, it helps for us to pray with Scriptures that invite us to deepen our understanding of God's love for us.

- Jeremiah 29:11–14 // "I know the plans I have for you . . . to give you a future with hope."
- Isaiah 43:1–7 // "You are precious in my sight, / and honored, and I love you."
- Psalm 139:1–18 // God's love at the source of my being; God's closeness to me
- Romans 8:31–39 // Nothing can separate us from the love of God.
- John 10:1–10 // "I came that they may have life, and have it abundantly."

Discernment is about being open to God's call and being free to hear God's call. In Ignatian spirituality, we call this *indifference* or *spiritual freedom*. Here are a few Scriptures that can help us open to God's ongoing, creative act of love and Jesus' call to follow him.

- Jeremiah 18:1–6 // Like clay in the potter's hands
- Isaiah 6:1–8 // "Here am I; send me!"
- Philippians 3:1–11 // "For [Christ's] sake I have suffered the loss of all things."
- Genesis 22:1–18 // Readiness to give all God asks
- 1 Samuel 3:1–10 // "Speak, LORD, for your servant is listening."

St. Ignatius invites us to contemplate the life of Christ when we are discerning, that we may have "an interior knowledge of our Lord . . . so [we] may love him more and follow him more closely" (SE #104).[35] Jesus gives us the model of what we are to do.

- Luke 2:22–39 // The presentation of Jesus in the temple
- Matthew 3:13–17 // The baptism of Jesus
- John 2:1–11 // The wedding feast at Cana
- Matthew 10:1–16 // The apostles sent out to preach
- Matthew 14:13–21 // The feeding of the five thousand

Finally, we are invited to look at what it means to be a true disciple of Jesus. What are the costs of discipleship? As the Scriptures show us, there is a cost to following Christ. It is called a narrow path for a reason. It is not easy to follow Jesus, who ends up carrying his cross and going through his Passion before his Resurrection.

- John 10:1–18 // Like the Good Shepherd who lays down his life for his sheep
- Matthew 16:24–27 // The cost to following Jesus
- 1 Corinthians 4:9–13 // Fools for Christ
- Philippians 2:1–11 // Having the mind of Christ
- 2 Corinthians 6:1–13 // Sharing in the cross of Christ

God also uses the gift of the Holy Spirit to help us wake up and pay attention to the invitations and calls.

---

35. George E. Ganss, SJ, *Ignatius of Loyola: The Spiritual Exercises and Selected Works* (New York/Mahwah, NJ: Paulist Press, 1991), 52.

Hearing God's Call

We can experience great angst when we yearn to know God's call for us but feel lost as to how to hear and understand that call. In the *Spiritual Exercises* we find a prayer for the grace to hear God's call: "I will ask for the grace I desire. Here it will be to ask of our Lord the grace not to be deaf to His call, but prompt and diligent to accomplish His most holy will."[36]

St. Ignatius helps us understand how the Holy Spirit speaks to us through God's longing for us within the movements of our heart. God longs to enter our lives and for us to accept the invitation to be in relationship with God. God longs to enter our brokenness and free us from sin. God also longs for us to say yes to his call.

As we continue on the path of faith, God raises desires within us to act in ways that correspond to the gifts we are given. God gives us not only the desires and the gifts but also the means and opportunities to act on them. Sometimes we feel restless, tired, and uneasy because we are simply not doing what God is inviting us to do. This might mean that we are not discerning the vocation God is asking us to pursue, or we might not be saying yes to an invitation to use our gifts or live out a call.

This type of restlessness is the kind I wrestled with when I was teaching and felt God calling me to say yes to full-time ministry. I felt like Jacob wrestling with the man in the dream as God was seeking to give him a new name and a new role (Genesis 32:23–33). When I finally acquiesced and said yes instead of no, my restlessness subsided. I met God's longing for me to respond.

---

36. St. Ignatius, *The Spiritual Exercises of St. Ignatius*, trans. and ed. Louis J. Puhl, SJ (Chicago: Loyola Press, 1951), #91.

This restlessness we feel might be God getting our attention and inviting us to say yes to an invitation. Notice any restlessness you might feel. Ask yourself,

- Is God inviting me to say yes to something and I am ignoring it?
- Is there a new call God is inviting me to tend to but I am afraid to pursue it?
- Might God be inviting me to use one of my gifts and I am not doing so?

If our restlessness is stemming from our no when God is clearly inviting us to say yes, then the disquiet within us will subside when we say yes. Maybe God is birthing a new call within us, and while we notice the nudge toward a new yes, we are saying no with our words and our actions. The gift of the restlessness is helping us know that God steps forward for us. Restlessness often calms when we step forward in faith and say yes to what God is asking of us.

LET'S GO TO THE INNER CHAPEL

Notice what you are noticing. That is one of my favorite lines, and I say it often in spiritual direction. I feel that discernment is about noticing. Noticing the promises of God at work in our life. Noticing the love given to us by God. Noticing the deep desires in our hearts to respond to the love given to us. Noticing the longings of other people. Noticing our gifts. Noticing the way God is inviting us to respond to the longings we see with the gifts we are given. Noticing the movements of the Holy Spirit. It is all about noticing.

We discover the unique call upon our lives when we notice the needs of the world around us and the gifts we have to respond to the needs. The great Frederick Buechner says it best: "The place God calls you to is the place where your deep gladness and the world's deep hunger meet." When we notice both the needs of the world and our gifts that give us joy and meet those needs, we have found our promised unique call.

I want to offer you two tools that help discover our callings. The first is a prayer tool that my friend and colleague Stephanie Clouatre Davis and I created to use in the retreat ministry we do together. This is a way to review your life and notice the unique gifts and callings God gave you. The second tool is the Examen prayer.

Tool #1: Discovering God's Unique Call for Me

Our yes to discipleship invites us to follow God in a unique way and to use our gifts in a unique way to help build God's kingdom. Pause and reflect on the unique way God has invited you to say yes to your call to discipleship.

- What theme(s) do I perceive about my life?
- In my day-to-day life, what really excites me, gives me energy? What do I really enjoy doing?
- In my day-to-day life, what drains me, makes me tired? What do I not enjoy doing?
- What do I yearn to do that I have not been doing? What do I sense is God's yearning and desire for me?
- What do I see as my gifts? My strengths? My growth points?

- What do others see as my gifts? My strengths? My growth points?
- In what ways have my faith community, my colleagues, my friends, and my family called me to use my gifts? How are they likely to call on me for help?
- Who has God uniquely given me to love?
- What jobs and tasks are mine to do? If I had to choose, would I say that I'm better at working with people, ideas, things, or information? A mix of these?

Tool #2: The Examen

According to Jean-Pierre de Caussade, SJ,

> Those who have abandoned themselves to God always lead mysterious lives and receive from God exceptional and miraculous gifts by means of the most ordinary, natural and chance experiences in which there appears to be nothing unusual. The simplest sermon, the most banal conversations, the least erudite books become the source of knowledge and wisdom to these souls by virtue of God's purpose. This is why they carefully pick up the crumbs which clever minds tread underfoot, for to them everything is precious and a source of enrichment.[37]

God works through our common, ordinary means, and we can "pick up the crumbs," as de Caussade suggests, along the way. God meets us in our busy lives and uses everyday things to help us learn about God and also discover our unique call. In discernment, the *examen* helps us "pick up the crumbs" of daily life in three ways.

- First, this prayer method can help us name our gifts.
- Second, it can help us name the desires of our heart.
- Third, it can give clarity on our next right steps.

Let's review the steps of the *examen* quickly: (For a full *examen* description, see page 114)

1. Ask for the Holy Spirit's help.
2. Be thankful.
3. Notice God's presence.
4. Notice the lack of God's presence.
5. Look to the future.

Each day, the *examen* invites us to see our day and ourselves as God sees them. The *examen* can help us notice our gifts and desires. As we review our day in prayer, we might thank God for a time we got to do something we enjoy, we are good at, and we are passionate about. We might notice whom we enjoy spending our time with and whom we do not. We notice activities and tasks that bring us life and those we cannot stand to do or those that drain our energy and decrease our faith.

If we pray the *examen* daily, we will begin to notice recurring patterns, and these will give us direction on what our next right step might be, which will ultimately lead to our living out the deepest desires of our hearts and making the concrete contribution God hopes we will give to the kingdom.

Embracing the Promises of God

These Scriptures can encourage you as you read them and pray with them.

- Romans 11:29 // "For the gifts and the calling of God are irrevocable."
- Acts 2:37–42 // "For the promise is for you, for your children, and for all who are far away, everyone whom the Lord our God calls to him."
- John 21:15–19 // Jesus affirms Peter's call.
- Romans 10:14–15 // "But how are they to call on one in whom they have not believed? And how are they to believe in one of whom they have never heard? And how are they to hear without someone to proclaim him? And how are they to proclaim him unless they are sent? As it is written, 'How beautiful are the feet of those who bring good news!'"

---

37. Jean-Pierre de Caussade, SJ, *The Sacrament of the Present Moment*, quoted in James Martin, SJ, *The Jesuit Guide to (Almost) Everything* (New York: HarperCollins, 2010), 284.

Epilogue: Reasons for Our Hope

Boppy was incredibly scared going into his first surgery in August 2016. Afterward, he woke up relieved to be alive, and he kept saying, "Becksa, thank the Lord. Thank the Lord." To which I would reply, "Yes, Boppy—thank the Lord!" He finally said, "No—thank *THE LORD*." Finally understanding what he meant, I invited us to pause as a family to thank the Lord for bringing him through surgery successfully. Throughout his journey, there were many other times we stopped and together thanked the Lord. Boppy's spirit of generosity and thanksgiving were an ever-steady source of hope.

After one of his later surgeries, he was so overcome with gratitude at being alive still. He kept asking over and over again, "How do I deserve this? How do I deserve the gifts of my life and all God has given me?" How often do we ask ourselves these same questions about God? How do we deserve what God has given us?

Many days, the realization of God's generosity leaves me speechless or not sure how to respond, but that day my grandfather's response to God's generosity came out in a prayer of thanksgiving; he belted out the lyrics to one of his favorite songs by Kris Kristofferson, "Why Me, Lord?" For those of you who have not heard this older country song, it is a song that expresses gratitude to Jesus for the blessings in life that we do not deserve and asks how we can repay Jesus for all he has done for us.

After singing it on his own, he invited me to join him, and before long we were both singing this song. I'll never forget the sheer joy and hope I felt in that moment, watching him sing as he embraced the gift of life, the gift of loved ones, and the gift of God's promises. It was a lived experience of what Jesus' resurrection means in our lives.

It didn't make sense to have hope that day, with all that we were facing, but God increased our sense of it and allowed the Good News to be proclaimed that day from the mouth of a man recovering in his hospital bed. Perhaps this is how the disciples felt as they first experienced Jesus' resurrection in the middle of their sorrow and grief. When the risen Christ appeared to them, it didn't make sense to them at first. They were startled and terrified (Luke 24:37). It took some time for them to understand that Jesus was *still* with them. Thomas even needed evidence of the marks from the nails in Jesus' hands to believe that Jesus was here, but when he finally understood, he cried out a profession of faith: "My Lord and my God!"

This was a profession-of-faith moment for Boppy. It was a moment of hope for me, too, when I wholeheartedly cried out with belief that "My Lord and my God" was near. I understood what St. Thomas Aquinas meant when he said that hope, one of our theological virtues, is infused in us by God alone. We were not hoping alone that day. We never were. The risen Christ was with us in the hospital room just as he had been with us every step of the way up to that point and through the end of Boppy's life.

Jesus is still with me and each one of us today. That's the hope of the Resurrection. We have so many reasons to rejoice. We can rejoice in Jesus' presence in our lives and in the generous promises he continues to abundantly share with us. As I write this, I cannot help but recall the line from Philippians that says, "Rejoice in the Lord always;

again I will say, Rejoice. . . . The Lord is near" (4:4–5). The Lord *is* near to every one of us. He is so near that he abides in our inner chapels and is inseparable from us. This is why we can hope. The Lord is still near.

The realization that day in the hospital that the Lord was near fired my grandfather even further in his mission of generosity the last few months of his life. Even when his left side weakened, he continued to love and give generously. Even when the infection in his brain could not be cured, he continued to share his gifts of love, time, and resources with those around him. Even when he was in his hospice bed facing the reality of life's end, he continued to respond generously to God's love for him by loving others.

I will never be the same because of the journey of walking with him and watching God accompany him. The witness of God's promises at work in those months solidified things that God had invited me for years to understand through life's experiences and so many times of prayer in my inner chapel.

St. Ignatius's closing meditation in the *Spiritual Exercises* is called the "Contemplation on the Love of God." It opens with two points.

> The first is that love ought to show itself in deeds over and above words. The second is, that love consists in a mutual sharing of goods. For example, as a lover gives and shares with the beloved something of one's own personal gifts or some possesions which one has or is able to give; so, too, the beloved shares in a similar way with the lover. In this way, one who has knowledge shares it with the one who does not, and this is true for honors, riches, and so on. In love, one always wants to give to the other. (SE #231–31)

Ignatius invites us to stand in the presence of God and all of God's angels and saints, who intercede on our behalf as we ask for what we desire: that we may have "an intimate knowledge of all the goods which God lovingly shares with me. Filled with gratitude, I want to be empowered to respond just as totally in my love and service" (SE #233). We are then invited to recall all the blessings and gifts God has given us. We are invited to reflect on how much God has done for us and given to us. In my mind, we are invited to remember and ponder the gift of God's promises that we come to understand through our time in the inner chapel.

That is what this book is about, really. A remembrance of all the ways God loved me and loves each of us. All the ways God poured promises into my life through that grace-filled portal I call the inner chapel. As the realization of God's promises came into clarity for me over the years, all I could do was stand in awe of what God who loves me shares with me. Love manifesting not only in words but also in deeds. God generously sharing with me and with those around me. So that what God has made known to me might help someone else understand the love available to them from God.

My grandfather understood this well. By no means was he perfect. What human is? Like all of us, he had his weaknesses, a short fuse at times, and areas in which he sought God's mercy and forgiveness until the end of his life. He possessed, though, a gratitude for the blessings of his life that I have never witnessed in another human being. The gratitude for what he had and understood propelled him to share it generously with others.

One of the unexpected gifts of walking with someone with brain cancer is having the time to ask your loved one questions and listen to all their stories with a more intentional ear to remember all the details. About ten days prior to his death, I asked Boppy what he considered his life's lesson and what he hoped to be his legacy. He told me, "Be giving . . . always be giving!" He went on to share how he wanted his grandchildren and great-grandchildren to learn how "to be generous givers and also how to graciously receive a gift."

On my grandfather's prayer card at his funeral, we put the lines from Proverbs that reads, "One gives freely, yet grows all the richer. . . . [and] whoever brings blessing, will be enriched" (11:24–25). My grandfather enriched lives through his generosity. He gave gifts to all freely without needing recognition. Everyone was of interest to him. He saw worth in all people and freely shared his time, his attention, and his resources. In his eyes, the mere fact that he had met you and he knew you meant you were the beneficiary of his freely given love and generosity.

Isn't this how it is with God, though? By the mere fact that God created us, God loves us. Because God loves us, God is generous in sharing God's promises with us.

Thankfully, people come along in our lives and offer their faith, their gifts, their love, and all they possess. We have many spoon holders! Many people held the spoon for me to understand the gift of the inner chapel and the promises of God. My grandfather was one of them and continues to be even though he's no longer physically here. My grandmother still is as she models a faith rooted in hope. I hope that I have at times been a spoon holder for them, too, offering the gifts of my life and reminding them of the promises of God in their lives.

Isn't this how it is for all of us? At some point, someone holds the spoon for us in regard to our faith lives. Showing us the ropes. Teaching us how to pray. All the while with the hope that we will know the tools one day to access on our own the spiritual food we long for. As we learn it, our role becomes feeding ourselves, helping others access the spiritual food, and also teaching others how to begin to do it. That's the spirit of generosity my grandfather modeled so well. It is what Jesus modeled, fully sharing himself with us. It is what Jesus asked Peter to do after the Resurrection. Let's look at this exchange of love.

> When they had finished breakfast, Jesus said to Simon Peter, "Simon son of John, do you love me more than these?" He said to him, "Yes, Lord; you know that I love you." Jesus said to him, "Feed my lambs." A second time he said to him, "Simon son of John, do you love me?" He said to him, "Yes, Lord; you know that I love you." Jesus said to him, "Tend my sheep." He said to him the third time, "Simon son of John, do you love me?" Peter felt hurt because he said to him the third time, "Do you love me?" And he said to him, "Lord, you know everything; you know that I love you." Jesus said to him, "Feed my sheep." (John 21:15–17)

Jesus invites Peter to put his love for Jesus into action. Jesus invites Peter to share what he has with those he loves. In essence, Jesus put the spoon in Peter's hands. Giving him the task of feeding others the Good News, the promises of God. That spoon, full of love, passed from Peter into other disciples' hands. In turn, they passed the spoon into others' hands, and on and on it continued until today, in this present moment. We now feast on what Jesus shared of himself so generously centuries ago. We hold and receive the gift of the inner chapel. We embrace the promises of God.

I close this book first with the promise that I will continue to be a spoon holder not only for the loved ones in my life but also for you. May you come to understand in a bone-deep knowing way what the lived reality of the promises of God can do in your life. May you go often to your own inner chapel and meet God there and discover the gifts and promises that await you.

I invite you to be a spoon holder with me, sharing what we have with those we love. May the love we receive from God turn into actions that invite others to take up the spoon and feast on the promises of God and share them with others. This is how the Good News continues to spread. This is how our world is transformed. Who needs to know the inner chapel exists? Who in your life needs to hear these promises?

What we understand about the life-changing gift of a relationship with God is not for us alone. What do we do with the gift of the inner chapel and the promises of God? Share them. Generously share. So many need this message of hope. I urge you to join me in carrying on my grandfather's spirit of hope, love, and generosity.

May we "Be giving . . . always be giving!"

Lord, teach me to be generous.
Teach me to serve you as you deserve;
to give and not to count the cost,
to fight and not to heed the wounds,
to toil and not to seek for rest,
to labor and not to ask for reward,
save that of knowing that I do your will.

—St. Ignatius

Acknowledgments

This book came into being through the love, support, and encouragement of family, friends, and colleagues. God sent an army of people who helped birth this book. Join me in thanking God for . . .

My grandfather John Perkins. Boppy, your love and belief in me until the very end is a gift that changed me forever. Thank you for your witness of generosity, hope, and love. May this book continue to share the impact your life had on me and on all who knew you. May it call us to carry on your legacy of generosity.

My grandmother Carolyn Perkins. "B," you are a steadfast witness of hope and faith to me. You make the best cup of coffee in the world, and there is no one else I would rather sit and talk about life with than you. Thank you for sharing the gift of faith with me and for showing me how to love.

My brothers (Chip Uffman and Connor Uffman), my sisters-in-law (Ashley Musick Uffman and Amy Holloway Uffman), and my beautiful nieces and nephews, I hope and pray that this book honors Boppy's impact on our lives. I am thankful for each of you and your ongoing love and support.

Mom and Dad, and the entire Uffman family, for helping lay in me a solid foundation of prayer and faith that I continue to build upon each day.

My grandparents' dear friends, Steve and Cindy Junot, Randy and Stacy Lemoine. My grandfather's niece Tiny Coker and her husband, Bill. Your presence, love, and companionship were gifts to not only my grandfather but also to our entire family during his sickness. Thank you for staying with us to the end.

Stephanie Clouatre Davis, one of my best friends and my partner-in-crime for retreat ministry. This book came to fruition because of you "getting" me. You helped me hear my own language about the inner chapel and the promises of God long before I did. Standing shoulder to shoulder with you in ministry is one of the biggest gifts of my life. Ministry is a lot less lonely and a lot more fun. Thank you for cowriting the meditation "Discovering God's Unique Call for Me." Your collaboration is felt in many other areas of this book also just by your friendship and our collaborative ministry in our local region. It's your turn now, my friend, to write and share what's in you!

The group of women I am privileged to call heart friends: Marcie Buckle, Missy Devillier, Christianne Squires, and Stephanie Clouatre Davis. You accompany me through life's ups and downs, making sure my feet are planted on the solid ground of faith. I am thankful not only for friendships with you but also my family's friendship with all of your families. Chris, Sydnie, Bill, Gaven, Collin, Ryan, Kirk, Michael, Emma, and Abby, thank you for being part of our "framily."

Joe Durepos, thank you for yet again challenging me to bring out nothing less than my best and for seeing something I did not see at first. When you told me to get a proposal together in three weeks, I thought you were crazy. You were right. It was in me way more than I realized. Your mentorship and friendship continue to inspire me to believe in my voice and writing.

Vinita Wright, your greatest gift to me on this book is understanding the ministry of retreat work and spiritual direction. You kept reminding me to lead with what I am called to do: accompany people.

I am in awe of how you took the words God poured out of me and arranged them in a way that makes complete sense for others to engage on a journey of faith. You are the voice our world needs to hear more from in regard to spirituality.

The entire Loyola Press family, especially Carrie Freyer, Denise Gorss, Joellyn Cicciarelli, Mandy Lemos, Joe Paprocki, Carol Dreps, Laura Trelese, Maria Cuadrado, Santiago Cortes-Sjoberg, and Dierdre Mullane.

My early readers: Claudia Maxson and Collin DeVillier. Claudia, our newfound friendship is a gift. Your accompaniment in being a reader along the way clarified many things, including the focus of this book. Collin, I want to listen to your intuition and wisdom every day of my life. Do not ever let anyone tell you that you are too young to impact our world and our church. Ann Funes, Kate Anderson, Caroline Lemann, and Jennifer Usher, thank you for your friendship and for reading various pieces and parts and sharing feedback.

Erica Kastner, for helping me with my blogs and themes that are now integral to this book. Charlotte Phillips, for your unbelievably detailed eye, and for helping me gather Scriptures for the end of every chapter. You helped me get this book across the finish line. Kathy Powell, for dreaming big dreams with me and inviting me outside my comfort zone constantly. I am glad we met all those years ago in Georgia. Faye Coorpendor and Melinda LeBlanc, for offering valuable insights from your own ministry as spiritual directors on different meditations in this book. Matt Gamble, for your friendship and wisdom to "cut the ballast." Fr. Michael Alello for your continued collaboration, brainstorming, and support in ministry.

Fr. Randy Cuevas, Fr. Eddie Martin, Aline Landry, and all the staff at St. Aloysius Catholic Church in Baton Rouge, for your hospitality and offering me writing space this summer to finish the book while my children were out of school. Chris and I are thankful for the community you provide our family.

Catherine Smith, Hannah Broome, Kelsey Murray, Debbie and George Eldredge (my amazing in-laws), for being with my kids at various moments, giving me time and space to write without interruptions. It truly takes a village to write a book, and I am thankful you were part of ours.

For all who have trusted me to accompany them either on retreats or in spiritual direction, know that this book would not exist without the space to walk with you and witness God's work in your lives. For the spiritual directors who accompanied me on silent retreats at Eastern Point Retreat House and also for Sr. Janelle Sevier, who accompanies me monthly in spiritual direction, you are profound witnesses of hope.

Brady, Abby, and Mary, I love you more than I can ever capture into words. Being your mom is the greatest gift of my life. You are wise and holy teachers of what it means to love like God and be loved by God. Thank you for your patience, support, and sacrifice in the creation of this book.

Chris, thank you for loving Boppy the way you did. You were a deep comfort to him in some of his darkest times. I learned so much about the kind of man you are by watching you love him. You accompanied me every step of the way as I accompanied him. You walked side by side with me as I wrote this book—cheering me on, encouraging me when I was discouraged, and picking up slack in areas of our family life so I had the space to write. I love you!

About the Author

Becky is an Ignatian-trained spiritual director, retreat facilitator, and author. She invites people deeper in their walk with Christ through facilitating retreats and days of reflection, writing, online retreat experiences, and spiritual direction.

Passionate about Ignatian spirituality and teaching people how to pray, Becky leans on her twenty years of ministry experience to help people make room for God in the busyness and invite them into deeper relationship with God.

Becky lives in Baton Rouge, LA, where she meets with men and women of all ages for monthly spiritual direction and leads people through the Spiritual Exercises of St. Ignatius. She directs in-person days of reflections and retreats, as well as online retreats to make the Ignatian retreat experience accessible to all, and is co-founder of the women's ministry, Women of the Well.

In addition, she offers weekly reflections on her own website, *www.beckyeldredge.com*, as well as reflections on Loyola Press' Ignatian Spirituality blog, dotMagis.

She shares life with her husband and three children.

Find additional resources from Becky Eldredge
on prayer and other spiritual practices at

www.loyolapress.com/eldredge

beckyeldredge.com

Also by Becky Eldredge

BUSY LIVES & RESTLESS SOULS

BECKY ELDREDGE

Even when you check every item off your daily list, do you still feel as though something meaningful and essential is missing from the very center of your life?

Spiritual director and writer Becky Eldredge has felt that same longing, and she knows what people are missing—a relationship with God through prayer. In the award-winning *Busy Lives & Restless Souls*, Eldredge interprets principles of Ignatian spirituality in a fresh way to equip us with prayer tools that are accessible and practical within the relentless realities of our daily routines.

For all who sense that there is a missing peace in their lives, *Busy Lives & Restless Souls* will help them find it—right where they are.

PB | 978-0-8294-4495-7 | $13.95

To Order:

Call **800.621.1008**, visit **loyolapress.com/store,** or visit your local bookseller.